WORKBOOK

# Focus on Personal Financial Literacy

High School Edition | 1st Edition

mheonline.com/honorselectives

WORKBOOK FOR FOCUS ON PERSONAL FINANCIAL LITERACY

Published by McGraw Hill LLC, 1325 Avenue of the Americas, New York, NY 10019. 

This book is printed on acid-free paper.

1 2 3 4 5 6 7 8 9 LHS 28 27 26 25 24 23

ISBN 978-1-265-63356-1
MHID 1-265-63356-8

# Contents

# Introduction

The *Focus on Personal Financial Literacy* Workbook was created to assist in engaging high school students with the importance of managing their current and future finances and goals. Activities and Flipped Classroom assignments are taken from real world scenarios to better aid student learning of the material in the Student Edition. The *Your Personal Financial Plan* sheets correlate with sections of the text and ask students to work thorough the applications and record their own responses. These sheets apply concepts learned to their unique situation and serve as a road map to their personal financial future.

# 1 Personal Financial Literacy: An Introduction





## Activity 1: Consumer Powers and Protections

**AS YOU READ,** learn the vocabulary. **AFTER YOU READ**, check your understanding through Fact and Idea Review, Critical Thinking Questions, an Extension Activity, and a Research Activity.

### What Are Your Rights as a Consumer?

Today, you can buy items using your computer, smart phone, or by going to a store. With the variety of options available, it is critical that you are an informed consumer so you can make good financial decisions. Fortunately, you have help and protections while shopping in today's marketplace.

In 1962, The Consumer Bill of Rights was established. It helps ensure that consumers can defend themselves against faulty or defective products. Consumers have a right to buy safe products and sellers have a responsibility to create and sell safe products. The four basic rights are a right to safety, to be informed, to choose, and to be heard. Consumers also have responsibilities. Your responsibilities as an informed consumer are to use products safely, to research and use information, to choose wisely, to contact your public officials about consumer issues, and seek **redress**.

In addition to the Consumer Bill of Rights, there are consumer protection laws to protect you from dangerous products, fraud, or discrimination. These laws protect you even if you are unaware of them. Just look at food labels in your kitchen.

The Fair Packaging and Labeling Act of 1967 required truth in packaging and labels to help consumers know what their food contains and to be able to compare products.

To see another example, look for the warning label on children's toys. The Child Protection and Toy Safety Act was passed in 1994. It prohibits the sale of dangerous products intended for sale to children and requires a warning label on toys with small parts.

If you are shopping for a credit card or a loan, you will appreciate the Truth in Lending Act. It requires creditors to report all costs associated with borrowing money in a standardized form. This allows consumers to compare credit charges and interest rates.

Laws are enforced by federal and state government agencies such as the Consumer Product Safety Commission and the Department of Agriculture. State offices have consumer protection divisions, too. Locally, you can contact your city or county government for consumer assistance. Private, nonprofit consumer groups such as Public Citizen and the local chapter of the Better Business Bureau (BBB) will also work to help you resolve consumer issues. You can file a complaint with the BBB and they will act as a mediator to help resolve the issue. These laws and agencies ensure that businesses sell safe products and provide redress for consumers. Your state's attorney general may also offer dispute resolution through **arbitration**. For example, some states have "Lemon Laws". If a consumer buys a new car and it has a serious defect that is not corrected by the seller within a certain time frame, then the parties can go to arbitration to decide if the consumer is due a refund.

### Vocabulary

**Redress** – remedy for a wrong or loss

**Arbitration** – a procedure in which a neutral person or panel listens to both sides of a dispute, weighs the evidence, and decides what action should be taken to resolve the dispute

### Fact and Idea Review

1. What skills are required to be an effective consumer in today's marketplace?

2. What influence do you as a consumer have on sellers?

3. What rights and responsibilities do consumers and sellers have?

4. What legal protections do consumer have?

5. What forms of redress do consumers have at the state and local level?

## Critical Thinking

1. Why do you think the Consumer Bill of Rights was created? Are consumer protections still necessary? What do you see as the next trend in consumer issues?

2. How do the consumer protections of the Fair Packaging and Labeling Act and the Food and Drug Administration impact individuals and your families? What do you think the next consumer trend in labeling will be?

## Extension Activity

If your verbal complaints are not heard by a retailer, your next step is to write a letter of complaint. Write a letter of complaint to resolve a consumer issue you have experienced. As a class, discuss what other forms of redress are available to customers. Discuss what rights and responsibilities consumers and sellers have.

### Research Activity

**Directions:** Research the following agencies and groups and write a brief description of how these groups help consumers. Identify if they are local, state, federal, or private agencies.

1. Consumer Product Safety Commission

2. Better Business Bureau

3. Consumer Union

4. Food and Drug Administration

5. Attorney General's Office

6. United States Department of Agriculture

Which of the consumer protection groups would you contact in each of these scenarios?

1. Contractors repaired your roof last week, but it leaks during a thunderstorm.

2. You purchased a toy for your nephew that breaks into many small pieces.

3. You purchased food that caused you to become ill.

4. You want to research a new digital camera before you buy it.

# Activity 2: The Decision-Making Process

**AS YOU READ,** learn the vocabulary. **AFTER YOU READ,** check your understanding through Fact and Idea Review, Critical Thinking Questions, and an Extension Activity.

### Making Decisions

When you have to consider a problem, it is helpful to be aware of the positive and negative factors influencing your decision-making process. Each decision you make will have consequences. In addition, the results may only affect you, or they may affect others. Before you make a decision, consider the impact it will have on you as well as others. **Critical thinking** is about applying reasoning strategies in order to make sound decisions. Evaluating information, discerning fact from opinion, and drawing conclusions based on relevant criteria are strategies that can help you make good judgments.

The decision-making process consists of six steps. This process will help you make decisions effectively. The first step in the process is to identify the decision. You need to know what your goal is and what the desired outcome will be.

Next you should list possible options. Gather information to work and develop alternative solutions to see which one might work best for you. You should think of as many options as possible.

The third step is to consider the pros and cons of each option. Listing the pros and cons for each alternative will let you see very clearly which alternative is not going to work and which might work. Also remember to keep in mind how each alternative might impact others.

Once you have done this, you are ready for the fourth step: choosing the best option. You should select the option that will have the most positive outcome. The fifth step is to act on your decision. Identify what you need to do and carry out your decision.

The final step is to evaluate your decision. Ask yourself: Did I make the best choice? How did my decision impact others? You should allow a moment of reflection to reinforce how you arrived at your particular decision to learn from what you have done.

The factors that influence your decision-making process are past experiences, biases, age, and personal relevance. If you have lost money buying a risky stock, then in the future, you may not choose a risky stock. **Bias** is a preference that might prevent impartial judgement and may influence your decision.

Your age can also affect your decision-making process. Older people may be more confident in their decision-making abilities.

Personal relevance refers to the fact that when you believe what you decide matters, you are more likely to make a decision. Take voting for example, if you really believe it matters who wins, then you are more likely to vote. Once you make your decision, you may regret it or be pleased with it; either of these feelings will influence you the next time you use the decision-making process.

## Vocabulary

**Critical thinking** – applying reasoning strategies in order to make sound decisions

**Bias** – a preference that might prevent impartial judgement

## Fact and Idea Review

1. What are some factors that influence the decision-making process?

2. What are the six steps in the decision-making process?

## Critical Thinking

1. How do the factors influencing the decision-making process have a positive and/or negative influence on decisions?

2. How might values of different cultures in other parts of the world impact the decision-making process? Provide example.

3. How might two people choose different paths in the decision-making process? What are some possible reasons for their decisions?

4. What do you think would happen if a person did not consider the impact of his or her decisions on others or did not consider alternative courses of action?

**Extension Activity**

Recall a time you had to make a big decision. Apply the steps of the decision-making process. How did factors have a positive or negative influence on your decision? Summarize your experience.

Name ______ Date ______ Class ______

# Personal Financial Data

**Purpose:** To create a record of personal financial information.

**Financial Planning Activities:** Complete the information requested to provide a quick reference for your personal data.

**Suggested Websites & Apps:** www.money.com, www.kiplinger.com, www.20somethingfinance.com

| | | |
|---|---|---|
| **Name** | | |
| **Birth Date** | | |
| **Marital Status** | | |
| **Address** | | |
| **Phone** | | |
| **Email** | | |
| **Social Security No.*** | | |
| **Driver's License No.*** | | |
| **Place of Employment** | | |
| **Address** | | |
| **Phone** | | |
| **Position** | | |
| **Length of Service** | | |
| **Checking Acct. No.** | | |
| **Financial Inst.** | | |
| **Address** | | |
| **Website** | | |
| **Savings Acct. No.** | | |
| **Financial Inst.** | | |
| **Address** | | |
| **Website** | | |
| **Banking, Money Management Apps used:** | | |

## What's Next for Your Personal Financial Plan?

- Identify financial planning experts (insurance agent, banker, investment adviser, tax preparer, others) you might contact for financial planning information or assistance.
- Discuss with other household members various financial planning priorities.

(Note: Be careful where, when and to whom you provide your Social Security and Driver's License information. This can lead to identity theft.)

Name ______________________ Date ____________ Class ________

# Setting Personal Financial Goals

**Purpose:** To identify personal financial goals and create an action plan.

**Financial Planning Activities:** Based on personal and household needs and values, identify current or future goals that require action.

**Suggested Websites & Apps:** thebalance.com, www.360financialliteracy.org, Personal Capital

YOUR PERSONAL FINANCIAL PLAN 2

## Short-Term Monetary Goals (less than two years)

| Description | Amount needed | Months to achieve | Action to be taken | Priority |
|---|---|---|---|---|
| Example: Pay off credit card debt. | $850 | 12 | Reduce spending on takeout food. | High |
| | | | | |
| | | | | |

## Intermediate Monetary Goals (two to five years)

| Description | Amount needed | Months to achieve | Action to be taken | Priority |
|---|---|---|---|---|
| | | | | |
| | | | | |

## Long-Term Monetary Goals (beyond five years)

| Description | Amount needed | Months to achieve | Action to be taken | Priority |
|---|---|---|---|---|
| | | | | |
| | | | | |

## Nonmonetary Goals

| Description | Time frame | Actions to be taken |
|---|---|---|
| Example: Set up files for personal financial records and documents. | Next 2–3 months | Locate vital personal and financial records; scan copies, set up online files for various spending, saving, borrowing categories. |
| | | |
| | | |

## What's Next for Your Personal Financial Plan?

- Based on a financial goal, calculate the savings deposits necessary to achieve that goal.
- Identify current economic trends that might influence various saving, spending, investing, and borrowing decisions.

Name ______________________ Date ____________ Class ________

# Achieving Financial Goals Using Time Value of Money

**Purpose:** To calculate future and present value amounts related to financial planning decisions.

**Financial Planning Activities:** Calculate future and present value amounts related to specific financial goals using a financial calculator, spreadsheet software, or an online calculator.

**Suggested Websites & Apps:** www.moneychimp.com/calculator, www.grunderware.com, www.calculator.net

## Future Value of a Single Amount

1. To determine future value of a single amount.
2. To determine interest lost when cash purchases are made.

(Use an online calculator, app, financial calculator, or Excel.)

| **current amount** | **future value amount** |
|---|---|
| $ ____ | $ ____ |

## Future Value of a Series of Deposits

1. To determine future values of regular savings deposits.
2. To determine future value of regular retirement deposits.

(Use an online calculator, app, financial calculator, or Excel.)

| **regular deposit amount** | **future value amount** |
|---|---|
| $ ____ | $ ____ |

## Present Value of a Single Amount

1. To determine an amount to be deposited now that will grow to desired amount.

(Use an online calculator, app, financial calculator, or Excel.)

| **future amount desired** | **present value amount** |
|---|---|
| $ ____ | $ ____ |

## Present Value of a Series of Deposits

1. To determine an amount that can be withdrawn on a regular basis.

(Use an online calculator, app, financial calculator, or Excel.)

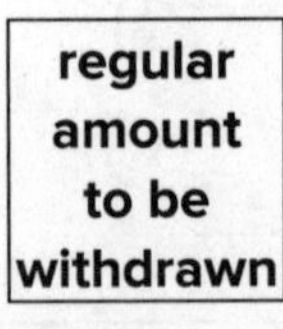

| **regular amount to be withdrawn** | **present value amount** |
|---|---|
| $ ____ | $ ____ |

## What's Next for Your Personal Financial Plan?

- Describe some situations in which you could use time value of money calculations for achieving various personal financial goals.
- What specific actions are you taking to achieve various financial goals?

# 2 Earning Income: Career Planning

YOUR PERSONAL FINANCIAL PLAN 4

Name ______________________ Date __________ Class ________

## Planning Your Career

**Purpose:** To become familiar with work activities and career requirements for a field of employment.

**Financial Planning Activities:** Complete the information required to provide you with more information about possible future careers.

**Suggested Websites & Apps:** www.monster.com, www.rileyguide.com, www.thebalancecareers.com, Job Search Organizer

| | |
|---|---|
| **Career job title** | |
| **Nature of the work**<br>General activities and duties | |
| **Working conditions**<br>Physical surroundings, hours, mental and physical demands | |
| **Training and other qualifications** | |
| **Earnings**<br>Starting and advanced | |
| **Additional information** | |
| **Other questions that require further research** | |
| **Sources of additional information**<br>Publications, trade associations, professional organizations, government agencies | |

## What's Next for Your Personal Financial Plan?

- Talk with various people who have worked in the career fields of interest to you.
- Outline a plan for long-term professional development and career advancement.

YOUR PERSONAL FINANCIAL PLAN 5

Name ______________________ Date ____________ Class ________

## Career Contacts

**Purpose:** To create a record of your professional contacts.

**Financial Planning Activities:** Record the requested information for use when researching career areas and employment opportunities.

**Suggested Websites & Apps:** www.linkedin.com, www.careerjournal.com, LinkedIn

| | | |
|---|---|---|
| **Name** | | |
| **Organization** | | |
| **Address** | | |
| **Phone** | | |
| **Website** | | |
| **Email** | | |
| **Date of contact** | | |
| **Contact situation** | | |
| **Contact's career situation** | | |
| **Areas of specialization** | | |
| **Major accomplishments** | | |
| **Name** | | |
| **Organization** | | |
| **Address** | | |
| **Phone** | | |
| **Website** | | |
| **Email** | | |
| **Date of contact** | | |
| **Contact situation** | | |
| **Contact's career situation** | | |
| **Areas of specialization** | | |
| **Major accomplishments** | | |

## What's Next for Your Personal Financial Plan?

- Identify people whom you might contact to obtain career information.
- Prepare specific questions to ask about career fields and career planning activities.

Name ______________________ Date ____________ Class ________

# Resume Planning

**Purpose:** To summarize your education, training, work background, and other experiences for use when preparing a resume.

**Financial Planning Activities:** List dates, organizations, and other data for the categories below.

**Suggested Websites & Apps:** www.monster.com, www.myperfectresume.com, https://resumegenius.com/, Resume Builder

## Education

| Degrees/programs completed | School/location | Dates |
|---|---|---|
| | | |
| | | |
| | | |
| | | |

## Professional Experience

| Title | Organization | Date | Responsibilities |
|---|---|---|---|
| | | | |
| | | | |
| | | | |
| | | | |

## Other Experience

| Title | Organization | Date | Responsibilities |
|---|---|---|---|
| | | | |
| | | | |
| | | | |
| | | | |

## Campus/Community Activities

| Organization/locations | Dates | Involvement |
|---|---|---|
| | | |
| | | |
| | | |
| | | |

## Honors/Awards

| Title | Organization/location | Date |
|---|---|---|
| | | |
| | | |
| | | |
| | | |

**References**

| Name | Title | Organization | Address | Phone |
|---|---|---|---|---|
| | | | | |
| | | | | |
| | | | | |
| | | | | |

**Note: See Exhibit 2-2 for resume format suggestions.*

## What's Next for Your Personal Financial Plan?

- Create a preliminary resume and ask others for suggested improvements.
- Conduct online research to obtain samples of effective resume formats and to avoid common resume mistakes.

Name ______________________ Date ____________ Class ________

## Cover Letter Planning

**Purpose:** To outline an employment cover letter.

**Financial Planning Activities:** Prepare the preliminary version of a cover letter for a specific employment position.

**Suggested Websites:** www.monster.com, www.resumegenius.com, www.thebalancecareers.com

YOUR PERSONAL FINANCIAL PLAN 7



| | | |
|---|---|---|
| **Name** | | |
| **Title** | | |
| **Organization** | | |
| **Address** | | |
| **Phone** | | |
| **Email** | | |
| **Information about employment position available** | | |
| **Organizational information** | | |

**Introduction:** Get attention of reader with an overview of how your background connects to the available position, mention of a person who recommended you for the position, a story that communicates some unique aspect of your background, or evidence of your desire to work in that industry.

**Development:** Emphasize how your experience, knowledge, and skills will benefit the needs of the organization in the future.

**Conclusion:** Request an interview, restate any distinctive qualities, and tell how you may be contacted.

**Note: See sample cover letter (Exhibit 2-3).*



### What's Next for Your Personal Financial Plan?

- Conduct online research for examples of effective cover letters.
- Prepare a preliminary cover letter and obtain comments for improvements from others.

YOUR PERSONAL FINANCIAL PLAN 8

Name ______ Date ______ Class ______

# Prospective Employer Research

**Purpose:** To obtain information about an organization for which an employment position is available.

**Financial Planning Activities:** Conduct research to obtain the information requested below.

**Suggested Websites & Apps:** www.careerbuilder.com, www.hoovers.com, www.annualreports.com, Job Search

Organization ______ ______
Address ______ ______
Contact ______ ______
Title ______ ______
Phone ______ ______
Email ______ ______
Website ______ ______
Title of position ______ ______

**Major products, services, and customers**

**Locations of main offices, factories, and other facilities**

**Major historical developments of the company**

**Employee benefits**

**Other comments**

## What's Next for Your Personal Financial Plan?

- Create a list of information sources to research prospective employers.
- Conduct online research about specific organizations in which you are interested.

Name ______________________ Date ____________ Class ________

# Interview Preparation

**Purpose:** To organize information and ideas for a job interview.

**Financial Planning Activities:** Prepare information for the items listed.

**Suggested Websites & Apps:** www.glassdoor.com, www.careerbuilder.com, www.careercontessa.com, 101 HR Interview Questions

YOUR PERSONAL FINANCIAL PLAN 9

**Organization** ______________ ______________

**Address** ______________ ______________

**Contact** ______________ ______________

**Title** ______________ ______________

**Phone** ______________ ______________

**Email** ______________ ______________

**Website** ______________ ______________

**Title of position** ______________ ______________

**Date/time/ location of interview** ______________ ______________

**Required skills and experience**

**Major responsibilities and duties**

**Questions you expect to be asked**

**Major ideas you plan to emphasize (main theme, stories of experiences)**

**Questions you plan to ask**

**Other comments**

## What's Next for Your Personal Financial Plan?

- Search online for commonly asked interview questions. Prepare preliminary answers for potential questions.
- Have others ask you questions in a practice interview setting.

# 3 Planning: Money Management and Budgeting

## Activity: Managing Your Resources

**AS YOU READ,** Learn the vocabulary. **AFTER YOU READ,** check your understanding through Fact and Idea Review, Critical Thinking Questions, and an Extension Activity.

**Budgeting to Meet Your Financial Goals:**

A **budget** is just a plan for controlling spending and encouraging **saving.** The purpose of a budget is to help you see what your income and spending looks like. Having a clear picture of how much money you have and what you spend it on will allow you to evaluate your habits and make better choices with your money.

A budget also lets you decide how much money you can afford to set aside for an emergency fund, and how much you want to save for future goals like school, buying a car or home, or taking a trip. To create a budget you need to estimate your income. This should be income after taxes, health insurance, and other deductions have been taken out. Then, estimate your expenses based on past spending or averages. Creating a line in your budget for savings may sound strange when your budget is mostly about spending. If you consider savings as another budget line item you will guarantee that you will have money saved for your future.

Most Americans spend the bulk of their budgets on housing, followed by transportation and food. Health care, life insurance, retirement, clothing, and entertainment make up smaller amounts of the typical American's budget.

**Discretionary expenses,** such as vacations, concert tickets, and sporting events, are often the first and easiest to cut from a bloated budget. Reducing food costs requires more effort, because you cannot live without food. Cutting coupons, buying generic brands, starting a garden, and not eating out are all ways to reduce your spending on food. Fixed costs like auto or health insurance can be harder to reduce but you can shop for cheaper car insurance, drive a less expensive car, or use your bike or public transportation. To add money to your budget, you or members of your family can work additional hours, work toward a promotion, or take on a second job.

A good budget can be adapted to your circumstances. If there is a life-changing event in your family, such as a job loss or a transfer to another state, your budget should be able to accommodate that. You may have to temporarily dip into your emergency fund, but eventually you should be able to go back to your revised budget and rebuild your savings.

Your budget should also address long-term goals, not just what you spend money on now. As an individual and a member of a family, you have goals like school or retirement. You have to plan for these events by setting aside realistic amounts of money in your budget.

## Vocabulary

**Saving** – setting aside money for future use

**Budget** – a plan for spending and saving based on income and expenses

**Discretionary expenses** – expense categories that are not absolutely necessary, such as vacations or entertainment

## Fact and Idea Review

1. What are some examples of individual and family resources?

2. What is the purpose and benefit of a budget?

3. What is the importance of having a savings plan?

## Critical Thinking

1. Explain how budgeting is critical to meeting financial goals. How do a budget and a person's financial goals impact other life goals?

2. How would you suggest a person should manage resources to meet his or her financial goals over a lifetime?

## Extension Activity

Come up with two short-term and two long-term financial goals. Research to find how much money you will need to reach these goals. Create a table to show the goals and what is needed to meet these goals. Now create a family budget to help you meet these financial goals. For your budget, you may use your family's expenses or research to find the average cost of typical expenses in your area. What are some areas in which you could reduce spending? Summarize how a person can better manage resources in a family budget.

| **Household budget** | |
|---|---|
| Mortgage/Rent payment | |
| Auto loan | |
| Auto insurance | |
| Auto expenses (gas, etc.) | |
| Groceries ($x/week) | |
| Utilities | |
| Phone Bill | |
| Medical | |
| Loan payment | |
| Life/Health insurance | |
| Vacation | |
| Entertainment | |
| Savings (college/retirement) | |
| Weekly Cash ($x/week) | |
| Total Expenses | |

## What are They Worth?

Learning Objective: Create and analyze a household's balance sheet.

### The Johnsons

The Johnson household has compiled the following financial information. They live in a house that has lost some of its market value due to zoning changes nearby; the best estimate for their house's worth is $150,000. While the Johnsons still owe $160,000 on their mortgage, they make payments of $1,200 each month. Groceries cost the family approximately $1,000 per month. The Johnsons also have a car (valued at $9,000; with loan balance of $10,870; monthly payments of $297), an SUV (valued at $15,900; with loan balance of $20,560; monthly payments of $498), and a boat (valued at $500; with loan balance of $2,210; monthly payments of $153). They have roughly $5,000 of furniture that includes mattresses, a couch, beds, an entertainment center, and several other items (they still owe about $1,670 on these items). Mr. Johnson is an avid baseball fan and has a card collection worth $1,400. Their credit card debt totals $15,000 with monthly payments of $485. To fund their higher education, the Johnsons took out some student loans that total $37,850 with payments of $276 per month. On average, the Johnson's checking account has $2,000, and their savings account has $3,700. Their combined retirement accounts have $21,009. Using the information above, complete a household balance sheet for the Johnsons in the space provided below.

| Assets | | | Liabilities | |
|---|---|---|---|---|
| Item | Amount | | Item | Amount |
| | | | | |
| | | | | |
| | | | | |
| | | | | |
| | | | | |
| | | | | |
| | | | | |
| | | | | |
| | | | | |
| | | | | |
| | | | | |
| | | | | |
| | | | | |
| | | | | |
| | | | | |
| Total Assets: | | | Total Liabilities: | |
| | | | | |
| | | | Net Worth: | |
| | | | | |

1. Perform a SWOT Analysis on the Johnson household and fill in your ideas below.

| Internal Factors | External Factors |
|---|---|
| Strengths | Opportunities |
| | |
| Weaknesses | Threats |
| | |

2. What financial advice would you give the Johnson family household to increase their net worth moving forward?

3. If you could ask three additional questions about their financial circumstances, what would you want to know about the Johnsons?

**4.** What does it mean to have a negative net worth?

**5.** List three major life events that would cause a household's net worth to decrease dramatically. Why would these events be problematic financially?

**6.** On average, would you expect a professional athlete to have a positive or negative net worth? Explain.

**7.** At what life stage would you expect the average person's net worth to reach its peak? Defend your reasoning.

Name ______________________ Date ____________ Period ________

# Financial Documents and Records:

**Purpose:** To develop a system for maintaining and storing financial documents and records.

**Financial Planning Activities:** Indicate the location of the following records, and create files for the eight major categories of financial documents.

**Suggested Websites & Apps:** www.kiplinger.com, www.usa.gov, FileThis, DropBox

| Item | Home file | Safe deposit box | Other (specify location – computer file, app, online) |
|---|---|---|---|
| **1. Personal/employment records**<br>- Budget, financial statements | | | |
| **2. Personal/employment records**<br>- Current resume, Social Security card<br>- Educational transcripts<br>- Birth, marriage, divorce certificates citizenship, military papers<br>- Adoptions, custody papers | | | |
| **3. Tax records** | | | |
| **4. Financial services/consumer credit records**<br>- Unused or canceled checks<br>- Savings, passbook statements<br>- Credit card information, statements<br>- Credit contracts | | | |
| **5. Consumer purchase, housing, and automobile records**<br>- Warranties, receipts, owner's manuals<br>- Lease or mortgage papers, title, deed, property tax info<br>- Automobile title<br>- Auto registration<br>- Auto service records | | | |
| **6. Insurance records**<br>- Insurance policies<br>- Home inventory<br>- Medical information (health history) | | | |

| 7. **Investment records**<br>- Broker statements<br>- Stock/bond records<br>- Rare coins, stamps, and collectibles | | | |
|---|---|---|---|
| 8. **Estate planning and retirement**<br>- Will<br>- Pension, Social Security info | | | |

## What's Next for Your Personal Financial Plan?

- Use an online program for storing your financial documents and records.
- Decide if various documents may no longer be needed; plan to shred.

YOUR PERSONAL FINANCIAL PLAN 11

Name ______________________ Date ____________ Period ________

# Creating a Personal Balance Sheet

**Purpose:** To determine your current financial position.

**Financial Planning Activities:** List current values of your assets; list amounts owed for liabilities; subtract total liabilities from total assets to determine your net worth.

**Suggested Websites & Apps:** www.kiplinger.com, money.com, www.thebalance.com, Personal Capital

## Liquid assets

Checking account balance ______________

Savings/money market accounts, funds ______________

Cash value of life insurance ______________

Other ______________

*Total liquid assets* ______________

## Household assets and possessions

Current market value of home ______________

Market value of automobiles ______________

Furniture ______________

Television, electronics, phone, computer ______________

Jewelry ______________

Other __________ ______________

Other __________ ______________

*Total household assets* ______________

## Investment assets

Savings certificates ______________

Stocks and bonds ______________

Retirement accounts ______________

Mutual funds ______________

Other __________ ______________

*Total investment assets* ______________

**Total assets** ______________

## Current liabilities

Charge account and credit card balances ______________

Loan balances ______________

Other __________ ______________

Other __________ ______________

*Total current liabilities* ______________

**Long-term liabilities**

Mortgage ______________________

Other __________ ______________________

*Total long-term liabilities* ______________________

**Total Liabilities** ______________________

**Net worth (assets minus liabilities)** ______________________

## What's Next for Your Personal Financial Plan?

- Compare your net worth to previous balance sheets.
- Decide how often you will prepare a balance sheet.

Name ______________________ Date ____________ Period ________

# Creating a Personal Cash Flow Statement

**Purpose:** To maintain a record of cash inflows and outflows for a month (or three months).

**Financial Planning Activities:** Record inflows and outflows of cash for a one- (or three-) month period.

**Suggested Websites & Apps:** www.americasaces.org, money.com, Spending Tracker, EveryDollar

For month ending ______________________

***Cash inflows***

Salary (take-home) ____________

Other income ____________

Other income ____________

***Total Income*** ____________

***Cash outflows***

***Fixed expenses***

Mortgage or rent ____________

Loan Payments ____________

Insurance ____________

Other ________ ____________

Other ________ ____________

Total Fixed Outflows ____________

***Variable expenses***

Food ____________

Clothing ____________

Electricity ____________

Phone/Cable/Internet ____________

Water ____________

Transportation ____________

Personal care ____________

Medical expenses ____________

Recreation/entertainment ____________

Gifts ____________

Donations ____________

Other ________ ____________

Other ________ ____________

Total Variable outflows ______

***Total outflows*** ______

***Surplus/Deficit*** ______

### *Allocation of surplus*

Emergency savings ______

Financial goal savings

Other savings ______ ______

## What's Next for Your Personal Financial Plan?

- Decide which areas of spending need to be revised.
- Use your spending patterns to prepare a budget.

Name ______________________ Date ____________ Period ________

# Developing a Personal Budget

**Purpose:** To compare projected and actual spending for a one- (or three-) month period.

**Financial Planning Activities:** Estimate projected spending based on your cash flow statement, and maintain records for actual spending for these same budget categories.

**Suggested Websites & Apps:** www.betterbudgeting.com, www.asec.org, www.mymoney.gov, Mint, YNAB

## Budgeted amounts

| ***Income*** | **Dollar** | **Percent** | **Variance** |
|---|---|---|---|
| Salary | | | |
| Other ____________ | | | |
| ***Total income*** | | **100%** | |
| ***Expenses*** | | | |
| Fixed expenses: Mortgage or rent | | | |
| Property taxes | | | |
| Loan payments | | | |
| Insurance | | | |
| Other ____________ | | | |
| Total fixed expenses | | | |
| Emergency fund/savings | | | |
| Savings for ____________ | | | |
| Savings for ____________ | | | |
| Total Savings | | | |
| Variable expenses: Food | | | |
| Utilities | | | |
| Clothing | | | |
| Transportation costs | | | |
| Personal care | | | |
| Medical and health care | | | |
| Entertainment | | | |
| Education | | | |
| Gifts/donations | | | |
| Miscellaneous | | | |
| Other ____________ | | | |
| Other ____________ | | | |
| **Total variable expenses** | | | |
| ***Total expenses*** | | **100%** | |

## What's Next for Your Personal Financial Plan?

- Evaluate the appropriateness of your budget for your current life situation.
- Are your budgeting activities helping you achieve your financial goals?

# 4 Planning: Taxes



## Activity: Tax Forms

**AS YOU READ,** learn the vocabulary. **AFTER YOU READ,** check your understanding through Fact and Idea Review, Critical Thinking Questions, an Extension Activity, and the Concept Application.

### Understanding Taxes

Taxes pay for many services that could not be paid for by any one individual or group. The federal government uses tax dollars to support Social Security, healthcare, national defense, and social services such as Supplemental Nutrition Assistance Program (SNAP, previously called "food stamps") and low-income housing. States, cities, and counties use tax dollars to build, operate, and maintain public schools, roads, prisons, garbage collection services, police and fire protection, and social services. By paying taxes, you are contributing to the greater good of your community and your country. If you knowingly do not file your tax returns, it is a criminal violation of the law. The Internal Revenue Service or IRS will audit your filings and compare your W-4 forms. They can collect the taxes owed, interest, and penalties. Tax policies provide benefits to families and individuals to offset certain expenses such as child care, education, and economic development. The child and dependent care tax credit gives a maximum $3,000 credit per child for working parents. The Hope Credit provides a maximum $2,500 tax credit for tuition costs to help pay for college. Businesses that invest in low-income communities receive tax credits to encourage them to build or start businesses and to employ more people. Most states also collect a state income tax. The states that do not collect an income tax tend to have higher sales tax or property tax rates. A tax year runs from January 1 to December 31, and you are required to file your federal income tax returns by April 15 each year.

**Amount***

Gross pay $1,923.08

Federal income tax $191.06

Social security tax $80.77

Medicare tax $27.88

State income tax $89.00

City income tax $57.00

Final pay check $1477.37

* Twice monthly pay based on 26 pay periods, annual income of $50,000.00

An employer is required to withhold federal, state and, in some cases, local income taxes from your paycheck. An employer will also have you complete a W-4 form which lets the employer know how many deductions you can take. A deduction can be a **standard deduction**, which deducts a flat rate per person claimed, or **itemized deductions** for interest on loans and charitable donations. For every deduction claimed, you deduct an amount of your income from being taxed. You can claim one deduction for yourself, one for a non-working spouse, and one for each child under the age of 18. States raise revenue in other ways, including sales taxes, excise taxes, license taxes, intangible taxes, property taxes, estate taxes, and inheritance taxes. Depending on where you live, you may end up paying all of these taxes or just a few of them. Property taxes are used to finance local schools, police, road repair, and other services. They are usually calculated by taking the assessed value of the home and multiplying that by the local tax rate. Applicable exemptions are then subtracted.

## Vocabulary

**Itemized deductions** on a tax return, a listing of the amounts actually spent on tax deductible expenses during the year.

**Standard deduction** on a tax return, a set amount that the IRS allows as a tax deduction without the need to list actual expenses.

## Fact and Idea Review

1. What are examples of local tax assessments?

2. Refer to the chart in the article to compute the local, state, and federal income taxes that the person in the chart pays in a year.

## Critical Thinking

1. Why is it important to file a yearly income tax return? What are the consequences of not filing?

2. How do federal, state, and local government tax policies affect individuals, families, and communities?

## Extension Activity

Research your local tax assessments. Create a chart or table showing how taxes collected in your community and state are allocated.

Name ______________________ Date ____________ Class ________

# Concept Application

## Review and complete the sample W-4 form.

### Form W-4 (2011)

**Purpose.** Complete Form W-4 so that your employer can withhold the correct federal income tax from your pay. Consider completing a new Form W-4 each year and when your personal or financial situation changes.

**Exemption from withholding.** If you are exempt, complete **only** lines 1, 2, 3, 4, and 7 and sign the form to validate it. Your exemption for 2011 expires February 16, 2012. See Pub. 505, Tax Withholding and Estimated Tax.

**Note.** If another person can claim you as a dependent on his or her tax return, you cannot claim exemption from withholding if your income exceeds $950 and includes more than $300 of unearned income (for example, interest and dividends).

**Basic instructions.** If you are not exempt, complete the **Personal Allowances Worksheet** below. The worksheets on page 2 further adjust your withholding allowances based on itemized deductions, certain credits, adjustments to income, or two-earners/multiple jobs situations. Complete all worksheets that apply. However, you may claim fewer (or zero) allowances. For regular wages, withholding must be based on allowances you claimed and may not be a flat amount or percentage of wages.

**Head of household.** Generally, you may claim head of household filing status on your tax return only if you are unmarried and pay more than 50% of the costs of keeping up a home for yourself and your dependent(s) or other qualifying individuals. See Pub. 501, Exemptions, Standard Deduction, and Filing Information, for information.

**Tax credits.** You can take projected tax credits into account in figuring your allowable number of withholding allowances. Credits for child or dependent care expenses and the child tax credit may be claimed using the **Personal Allowances Worksheet** below. See Pub. 919, How Do I Adjust My Tax Withholding, for information on converting your other credits into withholding allowances.

**Nonwage income.** If you have a large amount of nonwage income, such as interest or dividends, consider making estimated tax payments using Form 1040-ES, Estimated Tax for Individuals. Otherwise, you may owe additional tax. If you have pension or annuity income, see Pub. 919 to find out if you should adjust your withholding on Form W-4 or W-4P.

**Two earners or multiple jobs.** If you have a working spouse or more than one job, figure the total number of allowances you are entitled to claim on all jobs using worksheets from only one Form W-4. Your withholding usually will be most accurate when all allowances are claimed on the Form W-4 for the highest paying job and zero allowances are claimed on the others. See Pub. 919 for details.

**Nonresident alien.** If you are a nonresident alien, see Notice 1392, Supplemental Form W-4 Instructions for Nonresident Aliens, before completing this form.

**Check your withholding.** After your Form W-4 takes effect, use Pub. 919 to see how the amount you are having withheld compares to your projected total tax for 2011. See Pub. 919, especially if your earnings exceed $130,000 (Single) or $180,000 (Married).

### Personal Allowances Worksheet (Keep for your records.)

**A** Enter "1" for **yourself** if no one else can claim you as a dependent . . . . . . . . . . **A** ________

**B** Enter "1" if:
- You are single and have only one job; or
- You are married, have only one job, and your spouse does not work; or
- Your wages from a second job or your spouse's wages (or the total of both) are $1,500 or less.

. . . . . **B** ________

**C** Enter "1" for your **spouse**. But, you may choose to enter "-0-" if you are married and have either a working spouse or more than one job. (Entering "-0-" may help you avoid having too little tax withheld.) . . . . . . . . . . **C** ________

**D** Enter number of **dependents** (other than your spouse or yourself) you will claim on your tax return . . . . . . . . . . **D** ________

**E** Enter "1" if you will file as **head of household** on your tax return (see conditions under Head of household above) . . . . . . . . . . **E** ________

**F** Enter "1" if you have at least $1,900 of **child or dependent care expenses** for which you plan to claim a credit . . . . . . . . . . **F** ________

(**Note.** Do **not** include child support payments. See Pub. 503, Child and Dependent Care Expenses, for details.)

**G** **Child Tax Credit** (including additional child tax credit). See Pub. 972, Child Tax Credit, for more information.

- If your total income will be less than $61,000 ($90,000 if married), enter "2" for each eligible child; then **less** "1" if you have three or more eligible children.
- If your total income will be between $61,000 and $84,000 ($90,000 and $119,000 if married), enter "1" for each eligible child plus "1" **additional** if you have six or more eligible children. . . . . . . . . . . . . . . . . . . . . . . . . . . . . . . . . . . . . . . . . . . . . . . . . . . . . . . . . **G** ______

**H** Add lines A through G and enter total here. (**Note.** This may be different from the number of exemptions you claim on your tax return.) ▶ **H** ______

For accuracy, **complete all worksheets that apply.**

- If you plan to **itemize** or **claim adjustments to income** and want to reduce your withholding, see the **Deductions and Adjustments Worksheet** on page 2.
- If you have **more than one job** or are **married and you and your spouse both work** and the combined earnings from all jobs exceed $40,000 ($10,000 if married), see the **Two-Earners/ Multiple Jobs Worksheet** on page 2 to avoid having too little tax withheld.
- If **neither** of the above situations applies, **stop here** and enter the number from line H on line 5 of Form W-4 below.

---

**Cut here and give Form W-4 to your employer. Keep the top part for your records.**

| Form **W-4**<br>Department of the Treasury Internal Revenue Service | **Employee's Withholding Allowance Certificate**<br>▶ **Whether you are entitled to claim a certain number of allowances or exemption from withholding is subject to review by the IRS. Your employer may be required to send a copy of this form to the IRS.** | OMB No. 1545-0074<br>**2011** |
|---|---|---|

| **1** Type or print your first name and middle initial. | Last name | **2 Your social security number** |
|---|---|---|
| Home address (number and street or rural route) | | **3** ☐ Single ☐ Married ☐ Married, but withhold at higher Single rate.<br>**Note.** If married, but legally separated, or spouse is a nonresident alien, check the "Single" box. |
| City or town, state, and ZIP code | | **4 If your last name differs from that shown on your social security card, check here. You must call 1-800-772-1213 for a replacement card.** ▶ ☐ |

**5** Total number of allowances you are claiming (from line **H** above **or** from the applicable worksheet on page 2) **5** ______

**6** Additional amount, if any, you want withheld from each paycheck . . . . . . . . . . . . . . **6** $ ______

**7** I claim exemption from withholding for 2011, and I certify that I meet **both** of the following conditions for exemption.

- Last year I had a right to a refund of **all** federal income tax withheld because I had **no** tax liability **and**
- This year I expect a refund of **all** federal income tax withheld because I expect to have **no** tax liability.

If you meet both conditions, write "Exempt" here . . . . . . . . . . . . . . . . . . . . . ▶ **7** ______

Under penalties of perjury, I declare that I have examined this certificate and to the best of my knowledge and belief, it is true, correct, and complete.

**Employee's signature**

(This form is not valid unless you sign it.) ▶ Date ▶

| **8** Employer's name and address (Employer: Complete lines 8 and 10 only if sending to the IRS.) | **9** Office code (optional) | **10** Employer identification number (EIN) |
|---|---|---|

**For Privacy Act and Paperwork Reduction Act Notice, see page 2.** Cat. No. 10220Q Form **W-4** (2011)

Name ______________________ Date ______________ Class ________



## Deductions and Adjustments Worksheet

**Note.** Use this worksheet *only* if you plan to itemize deductions or claim certain credits or adjustments to income.

**1** Enter an estimate of your 2011 itemized deductions. These include qualifying home mortgage interest, charitable contributions, state and local taxes, medical expenses in excess of 7.5% of your income, and miscellaneous deductions . . . . . **1** $ ______

**2** Enter: { $11,600 if married filing jointly or qualifying widow(er); $8,500 if head of household; $5,800 if single or married filing separately } . . . . . **2** $ ______

**3** **Subtract** line 2 from line 1. If zero or less, enter "-0-" . . . . . **3** $ ______

**4** Enter an estimate of your 2011 adjustments to income and any additional standard deduction (see Pub. 919) . . . . . **4** $ ______

**5** **Add** lines 3 and 4 and enter the total. (Include any amount for credits from the *Converting Credits to Withholding Allowances for 2011 Form W-4 Worksheet* in Pub. 919.) . . . . . **5** $ ______

**6** Enter an estimate of your 2011 nonwage income (such as dividends or interest) . . . . . **6** $ ______

**7** **Subtract** line 6 from line 5. If zero or less, enter "-0-" . . . . . **7** $ ______

**8** **Divide** the amount on line 7 by $3,700 and enter the result here. Drop any fraction . . . . . **8** ______

**9** Enter the number from the **Personal Allowances Worksheet**, line H, page 1 . . . . . **9** ______

**10** **Add** lines 8 and 9 and enter the total here. If you plan to use the **Two-Earners/Multiple Jobs Worksheet,** also enter this total on line 1 below. Otherwise, **stop here** and enter this total on Form W-4, line 5, page 1 . . . . . **10** ______

## Two-Earners/Multiple Jobs Worksheet
(See *Two earners or multiple jobs* on page 1.)

**Note.** Use this worksheet *only* if the instructions under line H on page 1 direct you here.

**1** Enter the number from line H, page 1 (or from line 10 above if you used the **Deductions and Adjustments Worksheet**) . . . . . **1** ______

**2** Find the number in **Table 1** below that applies to the **LOWEST** paying job and enter it here. **However,** if you are married filing jointly and wages from the highest paying job are $65,000 or less, do not enter more than "3" . . . . . **2** ______

**3** If line 1 is **more than or equal to** line 2, subtract line 2 from line 1. Enter the result here (if zero, enter "-0-") and on Form W-4, line 5, page 1. **Do not** use the rest of this worksheet . . . . . **3** ______

**Note.** If line 1 is **less than** line 2, enter "-0-" on Form W-4, line 5, page 1. Complete lines 4 through 9 below to figure the additional withholding amount necessary to avoid a year-end tax bill.

**4** Enter the number from line 2 of this worksheet . . . . . **4** ______

**5** Enter the number from line 1 of this worksheet . . . . . **5** ______

**6** **Subtract** line 5 from line 4 . . . . . **6** ______

**7** Find the amount in **Table 2** below that applies to the **HIGHEST** paying job and enter it here . . . . . **7** $ ______

**8** **Multiply** line 7 by line 6 and enter the result here. This is the additional annual withholding needed . . . . . **8** $ ______

**9** Divide line 8 by the number of pay periods remaining in 2011. For example, divide by 26 if you are paid every two weeks and you complete this form in December 2010. Enter the result here and on Form W-4, line 6, page 1. This is the additional amount to be withheld from each paycheck . . . . . **9** $ ______

| Table 1 | | | | Table 2 | | | |
|---|---|---|---|---|---|---|---|
| **Married Filing Jointly** | | **All Others** | | **Married Filing Jointly** | | **All Others** | |
| If wages from **LOWEST** paying job are— | Enter on line 2 above | If wages from **LOWEST** paying job are— | Enter on line 2 above | If wages from **HIGHEST** paying job are— | Enter on line 7 above | If wages from **HIGHEST** paying job are— | Enter on line 7 above |
| $0 – $5,000 - | 0 | $0 – $8,000 - | 0 | $0 – $65,000 | $560 | $0 – $35,000 | $560 |
| 5,001 – 12,000 - | 1 | 8,001 – 15,000 - | 1 | 65,001 – 125,000 | 930 | 35,001 – 90,000 | 930 |
| 12,001 – 22,000 - | 2 | 15,001 – 25,000 - | 2 | 125,001 – 185,000 | 1,040 | 90,001 – 165,000 | 1,040 |
| 22,001 – 25,000 - | 3 | 25,001 – 30,000 - | 3 | 185,001 – 335,000 | 1,220 | 165,001 – 370,000 | 1,220 |
| 25,001 – 30,000 - | 4 | 30,001 – 40,000 - | 4 | 335,001 and over | 1,300 | 370,001 and over | 1,300 |
| 30,001 – 40,000 - | 5 | 40,001 – 50,000 - | 5 | | | | |
| 40,001 – 48,000 - | 6 | 50,001 – 65,000 - | 6 | | | | |
| 48,001 – 55,000 - | 7 | 65,001 – 80,000 - | 7 | | | | |
| 55,001 – 65,000 - | 8 | 80,001 – 95,000 - | 8 | | | | |
| 65,001 – 72,000 - | 9 | 95,001 –120,000 - | 9 | | | | |
| 72,001 – 85,000 - | 10 | 120,001 and over | 10 | | | | |
| 85,001 – 97,000 - | 11 | | | | | | |
| 97,001 – 110,000 - | 12 | | | | | | |
| 110,001 – 120,000 - | 13 | | | | | | |
| 120,001 – 135,000 - | 14 | | | | | | |
| 135,001 and over | 15 | | | | | | |

**Privacy Act and Paperwork Reduction Act Notice.** We ask for the information on this form to carry out the Internal Revenue laws of the United States. Internal Revenue Code sections 3402(f)(2) and 6109 and their regulations require you to provide this information; your employer uses it to determine your federal income tax withholding. Failure to provide a properly completed form will result in your being treated as a single person who claims no withholding allowances; providing fraudulent information may subject you to penalties. Routine uses of this information include giving it to the Department of Justice for civil and criminal litigation, to cities, states, the District of Columbia, and U.S. commonwealths and possessions for use in administering their tax laws; and to the Department of Health and Human Services for use in the National Directory of New Hires. We may also disclose this information to other countries under a tax treaty, to federal and state agencies to enforce federal nontax criminal laws, or to federal law enforcement and intelligence agencies to combat terrorism.

You are not required to provide the information requested on a form that is subject to the Paperwork Reduction Act unless the form displays a valid OMB control number. Books or records relating to a form or its instructions must be retained as long as their contents may become material in the administration of any Internal Revenue law. Generally, tax returns and return information are confidential, as required by Code section 6103.

The average time and expenses required to complete and file this form will vary depending on individual circumstances. For estimated averages, see the instructions for your income tax return.

If you have suggestions for making this form simpler, we would be happy to hear from you. See the instructions for your income tax return.

Review and complete the sample form I-9, which all United States employers must complete and retain for each citizen and noncitizen they hire for employment.

OMB No. 1615-0047; Expires 08/31/12

**Department of Homeland Security**
U.S. Citizenship and Immigration Services

**Form I-9, Employment Eligibility Verification**

**Read instructions carefully before completing this form. The instructions must be available during completion of this form.**

**ANTI-DISCRIMINATION NOTICE: It is illegal to discriminate against work-authorized individuals. Employers CANNOT specify which document(s) they will accept from an employee. The refusal to hire an individual because the documents have a future expiration date may also constitute illegal discrimination.**

**Section 1. Employee Information and Verification** *(To be completed and signed by employee at the time employment begins.)*

| Print Name: Last | First | Middle Initial | Maiden Name |
|---|---|---|---|
| Address *(Street Name and Number)* | | Apt.# | Date of Birth *(month/day/year)* |
| City | State | ZipCode | SocialSecurity # |

**I am aware that federal law provides for imprisonment and/or fines for false statements or use of false documents in connection with the completion of this form.**

I attest, under penalty of perjury, that I am (check one of the following):

☐ A citizen of the United States
☐ A noncitizen national of the United States (see instructions)
☐ A lawful permanent resident (Alien #) ____________
☐ An alien authorized to work (Alien # or Admission #) ________
until (expiration date, if applicable - *month/day/year*) ________

Employee's Signature

Date *(month/day/year)*

**Preparer and/or Translator Certification** *(To be completed and signed if Section I is prepared by a person other than the employee.) I attest, under penalty of perjury, that I have assisted in the completion of this form and that to the best of my knowledge the information is true and correct.*

| Preparer's/Translator's Signature | Print Name |
|---|---|
| Address *(Street Name and Number, City, State, ZipCode)* | Date *(month/day/year)* |

**Section 2. Employer Review and Verification** *(To be completed and signed by employer. Examine one document from List A OR examine one document from List B and one from List C, as listed on the reverse of this form, and record the title, number, and expiration date, if any, of the document(s).)*

| List A | OR | List B | AND | List C |
|---|---|---|---|---|
| Document title: ________ | | ________ | | ________ |
| Issuing authority: ________ | | ________ | | ________ |
| Document #: ________ | | ________ | | ________ |
| Expiration Date *(if any)*: ________ | | ________ | | ________ |
| Document #: ________ | | | | |
| Expiration Date *(if any)*: ________ | | | | |

**CERTIFICATION: I attest, under penalty of perjury, that I have examined the document(s) presented by the above-named employee, that the above-listed document(s) appear to be genuine and to relate to the employee named, that the employee began employment on** *(month/day/year)* __________ **and that to the best of my knowledge the employee is authorized to work in the United States. (State employment agencies may omit the date the employee began employment.)**

| Signature of Employer or Authorized Representative | Print Name | Title |
|---|---|---|
| Business or organization Name and Address *(Street Name and Number, City, State, ZipCode)* | | Date *(month/day/year)* |

**Section 3. Updating and Reverification** *(To be completed and signed by employer.)*

| A. New Name *(if applicable)* | B. Date of Rehire *(month/day/year) (if applicable)* |
|---|---|

C. If employee's previous grant of work authorization has expired, provide the information below for the document that establishes current employment authorization.

Document Title: ____________________ Document #: ____________________ Expiration Date *(if any)*: ______________

**I attest, under penalty of perjury, that to the best of my knowledge, this employee is authorized to work in the United States, and if the employee presented document(s), the document(s) I have examined appear to be genuine and to relate to the individual.**

| Signature of Employer or Authorized Representative | Date *(month/day/year)* |
|---|---|

FormI-9 (Rev. 08/07/09) Y Page 4

## What is Taxable?

Learning Objective: sort out taxable/nontaxable income streams and calculate taxable income

Emerson and Nevada, are both between career jobs. They are now married, and in order to make ends meet they are both working a number of part-time jobs and have some additional income streams. They sat down and made a list of everything they anticipate needing for tax season.

Emerson is still working part-time as a manager and makes around $3,105 per month before taxes are withheld. Emerson has invested $600 in an online business and earned of $1,200 in sales. He also bought around $500 in lottery tickets and won $100 early in the year. His student loans amount to $35,000, with a monthly payment of $277. Emerson received an email that he paid $2,170 in interest on his student loans in the past year.

Nevada is still working at her part-time job as an antique appraiser (10 hours per week at about $30 per hour; working roughly 42 weeks last year). The business-related mileage on her truck totals 6,800 miles. Many of Nevada's customers tipped her, so she earned an additional $5,780 in tips. She also profited $1,600 by selling a portion of her coin collection. Her savings account has earned $1.50 in interest, and her investments have paid her $576 in dividends. Last year Nevada graduated from her undergraduate program, and she paid $7,900 in tuition (she also qualified for the American Opportunity Credit). She is considering at going to graduate school to earn a master's degree soon.

For this example, we will ignore the possible presence of capital gains so you can group all the above forms of taxable income together along with any appropriate deductions to find this couple's taxable income. Ultimately, tax laws change every year so the key here is to get a general idea on how to treat these items. When it comes time to do their taxes, Nevada and Emerson should consult a tax professional.

**1.** List Nevada's and Emerson's income items in the table below, noting whether each item is generally taxable. Also list the tax deductions and credits and note whether they are refundable. Use the table to compute the couple's taxable income.

| Sources of Income | | | Tax Credits/Deductions | | | |
|---|---|---|---|---|---|---|
| Item | Amount | Taxable? | Item | Amount | Credit/ Deduction | Refundable/ Non-Refundable |
| | | | | | | |
| | | | | | | |
| | | | | | | |
| | | | | | | |
| | | | | | | |
| | | | | | | |
| | | | | | | |
| | | | | | | |
| | | | | | | |
| Total Income: | | | Total Deductions: | | | |
| | | | Total Refundable Credits: | | | |
| | | | Total Non-Refundable Credits: | | | |
| AGI: | | | | | | |

**2.** If the standard deduction is $12,600 for this tax year, is the couple better off using the standard deduction or itemizing their deductions? Why?

______________________________________________

______________________________________________

______________________________________________

______________________________________________

______________________________________________

______________________________________________

______________________________________________

3. Is there anything that Emerson and Nevada could do to shield more of their income from taxes? Explain.

4. Nevada is thinking about taking four years part-time to finish her master's degree instead of two years full-time. Would this option have any influence on their taxes?

5. Raising children can be very expensive ($17,000 per year on average). Should tax breaks be given for children or other dependents? Explain the type and amount of tax credits or tax deductions that you feel is most appropriate for dependent care expenses.

Name ______ Date ______ Period ______

# Federal Income Tax Estimate

**Purpose:** To estimate your current federal income tax liability.

**Financial Planning Activities:** Based on last year's return, estimates for the current year, and current tax regulations and rates, estimate your current tax liability.

**Suggested Websites:** www.irs.gov, TaxCaster, TaxSlayer

| | |
|---|---|
| **Gross income** (wages, salary, investment income, and other ordinary income) | $ |
| **Less** Adjustments to income (see current tax regulations) | −$ |
| **Equals** Adjusted gross income | =$ |
| **Less** Standard deduction **or** itemized deduction | |
| Medical Expenses (exceeding 10% of AGI) | $ |
| State/local income, property taxes | $ |
| Mortgage, home equity loan, interest | $ |
| Charitable contributions | $ |
| Casualty and theft losses (federally declared disaster areas only) | $ |
| **Amount −$** **Total** | **−$** |
| **Equals** Taxable income | =$ |
| ***Estimated tax*** (based on current tax tables or tax schedules) | $ |
| **Less** Tax credits | −$ |
| **Plus** Other taxes (AMT/Self-Employment Tax) | +$ |
| **Equals** Total tax liability | −$ |
| **Less** Estimated withholding and payments | −$ |
| **Equals** Tax due (or refund) | =$ |

## What's Next for Your Personal Financial Plan?

- Develop a system for filing and storing various tax records related to income, deductible expenses, and current tax forms.
- Using the IRS and other websites, identify recent changes in tax laws that may affect your financial planning decisions.

YOUR PERSONAL FINANCIAL PLAN 14

Name ______ Date ______ Period ______

# Tax Planning Activities

**Purpose:** To consider actions that can prevent tax penalties and may result in tax savings.

**Financial Planning Activities:** Consider which of the following actions are appropriate to your tax situation.

**Suggested Websites:** www.turbotax.com, IRS2Go



| | Action to be taken (if appliable) | Completed |
|---|---|---|
| **Filing status/withholding**<br>- Change filing status due to changes in life situation. | | |
| - Change amount of withholding due to changes in tax situation. | | |
| - Plan to make estimated tax payments (due the 15th of April, June, September, and January). | | |
| **Tax records/documents**<br>- Organize home files for ease of maintaining and retrieving data. | | |
| - Send current mailing address and correct Social Security number to IRS, place of employment, and other income sources. | | |
| **Annual tax activities**<br>- Be certain all needed data and current tax forms are available well before deadline. | | |
| - Research tax code changes and uncertain tax areas. | | |
| **Tax-savings actions**<br>- Consider tax-exempt and tax-deferred investments. | | |
| - If you expect to have the same or a lower tax rate next year, accelerate deductions into the current year. | | |

| | | |
|---|---|---|
| - If you expect to have the same or a lower tax rate next year, delay the receipt of income until next year. | | |
| - If you expect to have a higher tax rate next year, delay deductions since they will have a greater benefit. | | |
| - If you expect to have a higher tax rate next year, accelerate the receipt of income to have it taxed at the current lower rate. | | |
| - State or increase use of tax-deferred retirement plans. | | |
| - Other | | |

**What's Next for Your Personal Financial Plan?**

- Identify saving and investing decisions that could minimize future income taxes.
- Develop a plan for actions to take related to your current and future tax situation.

# 5 Saving: Banking and Financial Services

## Activity: Savings

**AS YOU READ,** learn the vocabulary. **AFTER YOU READ,** check your understanding through Fact and Idea Review, Critical Thinking Questions, and an Extension Activity.

**Understanding Your Savings Options:**

It is never too soon to start saving. You can start now by saving for your education using an education savings plan. Every state sponsors 529 savings plans, which are mutual funds that allow a yearly contribution to grow tax free. Each state determines the allowed yearly maximum contribution. About half of the states also allow a tax deduction on contributions to 529 plans. Anyone can contribute – parents, grandparents, aunts, uncles, and friends. It takes as little as $25 to start a 529 plan. Because 529 savings plans are mutual funds, there is a fee to manage the growth of the money, which ranges from 0–2.5 percent. For example, if you invest $10,000 and the expense ratio is 1.5 percent, then you play $150 that year. The 529 prepaid plan allows you to prepay some or all of the tuition costs, at today's price, and then cash the plan in later when you are ready to start school. The prepaid plan has restrictions if you use the plan for an out-of-state college.

Another option for saving for college is the Coverdell Education Savings Account. This account can be used to pay for college and graduate school, but it can also be used to pay for elementary and high school. The maximum yearly contribution is $2,000, which can grow tax free; it is not tax deductible. Parents, family members, and you can contribute to it. The money is invested in stocks, bonds, and mutual funds.

Another way to save money is to use a savings account. If you are only saving money for a short period of time or for emergency purposes for your budget, then a savings account will allow you easy access to your money. Savings accounts usually require a minimum balance and charge a fee if you go below it. The interest rates are usually low, under 2 percent.

When your goals are long term, it is best to save your money in places that are not easy to access, especially when the main reason is to save it. Long-term savings options include:

- A **money market account** is good for long-term goals because it has a much higher interest rate compared to a savings account. Once you build up enough savings, you might want to consider opening a money market account. The rate is higher if your balance is larger.

- A **certificate of deposit (CD)** places your money "on loan" to the bank for a period of time ranging from one month to five years while it earns interest for you. You cannot access your money until the time period is up without paying a stiff penalty.

- **Savings bonds** are backed by the United States Treasury and the interest you earn is tax-deferred. This means you will not pay taxes on it until you cash the savings bonds.

Most financial institutions use compounding interest to calculate earnings. Few use **simple interest.** Most banks pay compound interest. Compound interest is interest calculated on deposits you make and on the interest you have already earned. The more frequently interest is compounded, and the longer you leave your money in the account, the more you will gain. When comparing interest rates from several banks, make sure to take note of the annual percentage yield (APY). The APY tells you how much you will earn including the impact of compound interest. An example of compounding interest in action is if you deposit $1,000 at 10 percent compounding interest then the interest earned in the first month is $100. This interest is added to your original amount to equal $1,100. Next month's 10 percent interest earned will be on the new total of $1,100, which will increase to $1,210.

If you are evaluating investments for your money, the Rule of 72 is a quick and simple method to help you estimate the time it will take for an investment to double. You divide the interest rate into 72 to determine the number of years in which money will double. For example, $1 invested at a rate of 10 percent will take 7.2 years to double to $2. This is why exploring several banks and comparing the rates they offer is so important.

The SMART method (Specific, Measurable, Attainable, Relevant, Timely) is another way to help you create a financial plan with achievable results. You can use this method to set personal financial goals, such as planning for a large purchase, saving for college, or saving for retirement. **S**pecific refers to setting clear goals. A specific goal is more likely to be accomplished. For example, your goals should not be "save for a new car." Instead, the goals should be "save $500 a month for five months." **M**easurable refers to establishing an outcome for your goals. You should be able to measure the progress of your goal. You should set target dates and keep track of your progress. **A**ttainable means you should set your goals within reach. Identify goals that are most important to you. If the goal is important to you, you are more likely to achieve this goal. **R**elevant means that the goal should make sense to you. This step also stresses making your goals realistic. Only you know if a goal is realistic for you, but you should make sure to set realistic time frames for your goals. **T**imely means you should set a deadline to achieve your goal. A deadline will help to keep you focused on a track. An example of a SMART goal is as follows: You want to save to purchase a new computer, which will cost $600. While working a summer job, you plan to save $150 each month for four months. Your deadline is the last day of summer, which is when your job ends.

No matter how you save money, saving money is critical to meeting your short- and long-term financial goals. People today are living longer, so it is more important than ever to save and invest to prepare for your future and retirement. The choices you make now can impact your financial future. The options described in the article are just a few of the savings options available to you.

## Vocabulary

**Simple interest** interest calculated only on money deposited, not on prior interest earned

**Compound interest** interest calculated on both deposits made and prior interest earned

**Money market account** a type of savings account in which deposits are invested by the financial institution to yield higher earnings

**Certificate of deposit (CD)** a certificate issued by a financial institution to indicate the money has been deposited for a certain term

**Savings bonds** nontransferable debt certificates issued by the U.S. Treasury



## Fact and Idea Review

1. What are some long-term savings options? What are the benefits and drawbacks of long-term options?

2. What are some ways to save money for education? What are the drawbacks of each?

3. What is the rule of 72?

4. Why is it important to save money?

## Critical Thinking

1. Use the SMART method to set a short-term goal and a long-term goal. Remember to make your goal: Specific, Measurable, Attainable, Relevant, and Timely.

2. Evaluate the methods of saving money that are relevant to your goals. Which options would work best for you and your goals?

## Extension Activity

Research the characteristics of the savings options from the article in your areas or state. Include any additional options you discover. Create a chart displaying the characteristics of each savings option. Make sure to include specific details, such as terms, interest rates, and fees, as well as benefits and drawbacks of each. Finally, explain how each savings option relates to your short- and long-term financial goals.

Name ______ Date ______ Period ______

# Planning the Use of Financial Services

**Purpose:** To report current and future financial services.

**Financial Planning Activities:** List (1) currently used services with financial institution information (name, address, phone, website), and (2) services that may be needed in the future.

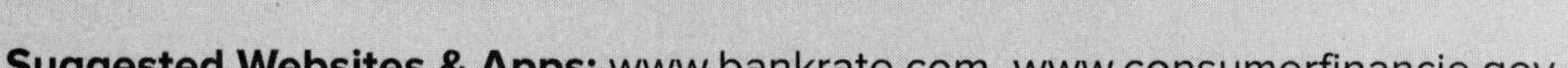

**Suggested Websites & Apps:** www.bankrate.com, www.consumerfinancie.gov

| Types of financial services | Current financial services used | Additional financial services needed |
|---|---|---|
| Payment services (checking, debit card, online payments, apps) | Financial Institution:<br>Address:<br>Phone:<br>Website: | |
| Savings services (savings account, money market account, certificate of deposit, savings bonds) | Financial Institution:<br>Address:<br>Phone:<br>Website: | |
| Credit services (credit cards, personal loans, mortgage) | Financial Institution:<br>Address:<br>Phone:<br>Website: | |
| Other financial services (investments, trust account, tax planning, apps) | Financial Institution:<br>Address:<br>Phone:<br>Website: | |

## What's Next for Your Personal Financial Plan?

- Assess whether the current types and sources of your financial services are appropriate.
- Determine additional financial services you may wish to use in the future.

16

YOUR PERSONAL FINANCIAL PLAN

Name ______________________ Date ____________ Period ________

## Comparing Saving Plans

**Purpose:** To compare the costs and benefits of different savings plans.

**Financial Planning Activities:** Obtain online information for financial service providers for the information requested below.

**Suggested Websites & Apps:** www.lbankrate.com, www.nerdwallet.com, Digit

| | | | |
|---|---|---|---|
| **Type of savings plan** (regular savings account, certificates of deposit, interest-earning checking accounts, money market accounts and funds, U.S. savings bonds) | | | |
| Financial service provider | | | |
| Address/phone | | | |
| Website | | | |
| Annual interest rate | | | |
| Annual percentage yield (APY) | | | |
| Frequency of compounding | | | |
| Insured by FDIC, NCUA, other | | | |
| Maximum amount insured | | | |
| Minimum initial deposit | | | |
| Minimum time period savings must be on deposit | | | |
| Penalties for early withdrawal | | | |
| Service charges/transaction fees, other costs/fees; limit on number of transactions per month | | | |
| Additional services, other information | | | |

### What's Next for Your Personal Financial Plan?

- Based on this savings plan analysis, determine the best types of savings plans for your current and future financial situations.
- When analyzing savings plans, what factors should you carefully investigate?

Name ______ Date ______ Period ______

# Savings to Achieve Financial Goals

**Purpose:** To monitor savings for achieving financial goals.

**Financial Planning Activities:** Record savings plan information along with the balance on a period basis.

**Suggested Websites & Apps:** www.savingsbonds.gov, www.fdic.gov, maxmyinterest.com, My Piggy Bank Savings Tracker

| Regular savings account | Savings goal/Amount needed/Date needed | |
|---|---|---|
| Acct. no. | Savings goal:<br>Date:______ | Balance:<br>$______ |
| Financial institution | Date:______ | $______ |
| Address | Date:______ | $______ |
| Phone | Date:______ | $______ |
| Website | Date:______ | $______ |

| Certificate of deposit | Savings goal/Amount needed/Date needed | |
|---|---|---|
| Acct. no. | Savings goal:<br>Date:______ | Balance:<br>$______ |
| Financial institution | Date:______ | $______ |
| Address | Date:______ | $______ |
| Phone | Date:______ | $______ |
| Website | Date:______ | $______ |

| Money market fund/acct. | Savings goal/Amount needed/Date needed | |
|---|---|---|
| Acct. no. | Savings goal:<br>Date:______ | Balance:<br>$______ |
| Financial institution | Date:______ | $______ |
| Address | Date:______ | $______ |

| | | |
|---|---|---|
| Phone | Date:__________ | $__________ |
| Website | Date:__________ | $__________ |

| **U.S. savings bonds** | **Savings goal/Amount needed/Date needed** | |
|---|---|---|
| Purchase location | Purchase date:__________ | Maturity date:__________ |
| | Amount:__________ | |
| Address | Purchase date:__________ | Maturity date:__________ |
| Phone | Amount:__________ | |
| Website | | |

| **Other savings** | **Savings goal/Amount needed/Date needed** | |
|---|---|---|
| Acct. no. | Initial deposit:<br>Balance:<br>Date__________ | $__________ |
| Financial institution | Initial deposit:<br>Balance:<br>Date__________ | $__________ |
| Address | Initial deposit:<br>Balance:<br>Date__________ | $__________ |
| Phone | Initial deposit:<br>Balance:<br>Date__________ | $__________ |
| Website | Initial deposit:<br>Balance:<br>Date__________ | $__________ |

## What's Next for Your Personal Financial Plan?

- Measure your current progress toward achieving various savings goals. Evaluate existing and new savings goals.
- Plan actions to expand the amount you are saving for financial goals.

Name ______________________ Date ____________ Period ________

# Comparing Payment Methods: Bank Reconciliation

**Purpose:** (1) To compare different payment accounts. (2) To determine the adjusted cash balance for your checking account.

**Financial Planning Activities:** (1) Compare checking accounts and payment services at various financial institutions (banks, savings and loan associations, credit unions, online banks). (2) Enter data from your bank statement and checkbook for the amounts requested.

**Suggested Websites & Apps:** www.bankrate.com, www.kipling.com, www.findabetterbank.com, MoneyPass (ATM locator)

| Financial Service Provider | | | |
|---|---|---|---|
| Address | | | |
| Phone | | | |
| Website | | | |
| Type of account (regular checking, activity account, bill payment service) | | | |
| Minimum balance | | | |
| Monthly charge below balance | | | |
| "Free" checking for students? | | | |
| Online banking services, mobile app banking | | | |
| Branch/ATM locations | | | |
| Banking hours | | | |
| **Other fees/costs** | | | |
| Printing of checks | | | |
| Stop-payment order | | | |
| Overdrawn account | | | |
| Certified check | | | |
| ATM, other charges | | | |
| Other information | | | |

# Checking Account Reconciliation

| | | | |
|---|---|---|---|
| Statement date: | **Statement Balance** | | $________ |
| **Step 1:** Compare the checks and payments with those paid on statement. *Subtract* the total checks written, payments, withdrawals not on the bank balance. | Check no. | Amount | –$________ |
| | | | |
| | | | |
| **Step 2:** Determine whether any deposits made are not on the statement; *add* the amount of the outstanding deposits to the *bank statement balance.* | Deposit date | Amount | +$________ |
| | **Adjusted Balance** | | =$________ |
| | | | |
| | **Checkbook Balance** | | |
| **Step 3:** *Subtract* fees or charges on the bank statement and ATM withdrawals from your *checkbook balance.* | Item | Amount | –$________ |
| | | | |
| **Step 4:** *Add* interest or direct deposits earned to your *checkbook balance.* | | | +$________ |
| Note: At this point, the two adjusted balances should be the same. If not, carefully check your math and make sure that deposits and checks recorded in your checkbook and on your statement are for the correct amounts. | **Adjusted Balance** | | =$________ |

# 6 Managing Credit: Sources and Uses



## Activity: Credit Cards

**AS YOU READ,** learn the vocabulary. **AFTER YOU READ,** check your understanding through Fact and Idea Review, Critical Thinking Questions, an Extension Activity, and a Concept Application.

### Understanding Consumer Credit

Before credit cards were commonplace, people would put an item they wanted to buy but could not afford immediately on "layaway." The store would keep the item until the customer paid for it in full. Now people rely on credit cards to pay for many items.

The typical credit card account is also called a revolving agreement because consumers make full or partial monthly payments to creditors. Other types of credit include charge cards, or interest-free plans, which are agreements between consumers and businesses in which consumers pay the monthly balance in full with no interest charged to them. An installment agreement is a signed contract to repay a fixed amount in equal payments over a specific period of time, such as 90 days. Automobiles or large appliances are often purchased this way.

All credit card application forms have something called a Schumer box. This feature was named after New York Congressman Charles Schumer, who sponsored legislation in 1988 mandating all credit card applications to clearly display the basic terms of the agreement. All boxes look similar and contain information about the annual fee, the Annual Percentage Rate (APR), other APRS (Balance transfer, cash advances, default APRs), the grace period, finance calculation method, and other transaction fees (balance transfer fees, late payment feess, over-the-limit fees.)

Some credit cards come with annual fees, which are fixed fees that must be paid each year. The APR is the cost of credit as a yearly interest rate, which is essentially a charge for using the credit card. Low interest credit cards are the better choice if you do not plan to pay the full amount each month. All credit cards come with a credit limit, which is the maximum balance the card can hold at any time. Even if you do not intend to pay off a credit card in full each billing cycle, you are required to send a minimum payment each month. The minimum monthly payment amount is calculated as a percentage of the total balance.

Many credit cards allow a grace period of 20 to 25 days before additional interest rates are applied. If you pay the balance on your credit card within the grace period, you can aviod paying interest on your purchases. Other credit cards have a double billing cycle. If you pay the balance in full one month but only partially the following month, you will be charged interest on both months. One other thing to keep in mind is that if you are reported for making late or missed payments by one creditor, your APR can be raised with your other creditors under the universal default clause. Some credit cards also charge fees for credit limit increases and other services.

Be careful of credit card offers with no annual fee; the APR interest rates could be higher on these cards. Credit cards that offer rewards such as cash back or points toward free airplane tickets might have other fees. Some cards offer a promotional interest rate that expires after six months or a year; learn the details of the promotion and what the new APR will be after the promotional period ends. Read the Schumer box closely to protect your finances and your future.

### Vocabulary

**Credit** the provision of money, goods, or services in exchange for the promise of future payment

**Creditor** a business or organization that provides credit

**Credit limit** the maximum amount of credit that a creditor will provide to a borrower

### Fact and Idea Review

1. What are some forms of credit?

______________________________________________

______________________________________________

______________________________________________

______________________________________________

2. What are the differences among credit plans such as revolving charge, 90-day and installment accounts, and interest free credit plans?

______________________________________________

______________________________________________

______________________________________________

______________________________________________

## Critical Thinking

1. What are the responsibilities involved with having a credit card? Why is it important to use your credit card responsibly? What are the consequences of not using credit responsibly?

2. What should you be wary of when shopping for credit cards?

3. Why do you need to understand the terms of a credit card?

## Extension Activity

Review the sample credit card statement. Locate the billing period for this statement, the annual percentage rate (APR), the payment due date, and the minimum payment due. Use the information in the Schumer box on page 62 and find two other credit card offers online to compare the annual fees, APR rates (including balance transfers), grace periods, and other transaction fees (including late payments, minimum finance charge, and cash advances). Create a spreadsheet showing your findings.

**Statement Date**
02/03/– –
**Payment Date**
02/28/– –

## CREDIT CARD STATEMENT

**Summary of Account Activity**

| Previous Balance | Payments | Purchases | Balance Transfers | Cash Advances | Past Due Amount | Fees Charged | Interest Charged | New Balance | Credit Limit | Available Credit | Statement Closing Date | Days in Billing Cycle |
|---|---|---|---|---|---|---|---|---|---|---|---|---|
| $535.07 | $450.00 | $240.60 | $0.00 | $0.00 | $0.00 | $0.00 | $1.13 | $332.80 | $1,000.00 | $667.20 | 2/28/20XX | 30 |

Questions?

Call Customer Service 1-xxx-xxx-xxxx
Lost or Stolen Credit Card 1-xxx-xxx-xxxx

**Payment Information**

| New Balance | Minimum Payment Due | Payment Due Date |
|---|---|---|
| $332.80 | $15.00 | 2/20/2010 |

**Late Payment Warning** If we do not receive your minimum payment by the date listed above, you may have to pay a $35 late fee and your APRs may be increased up to the Penalty APR of 28.99%.

**Minimum Payment Warning** If you make only the minimum payment each period, you will pay more in interest and it will take you longer to pay off your balance.

| If you make no additional charges using this card and each month you pay ... | You will pay off the balance shown on this statement in about ... | And you will end up paying an estimated total of ... |
|---|---|---|
| Only the minimum payment | 6 months | $89.04 |
| $40 | 3 months | $86.91 (Savings = $2.13) |

**SEND PAYMENTS TO: BANKCENTER P.O. BOX 6575 GOLDEN, NEVADA 88777**

| Sale Date | Post Date | Reference Number | Type of Activity | Location | Amount |
|---|---|---|---|---|---|
| 01/05 | 01/07 | 24036215006661 | Daisy Market | Clover, IL | 104.30 |
| 01/08 | 01/10 | 24692165008000 | Chloe's Coffee | Fielding, CT | 2.30 |
| 01/13 | 01/13 | 74046585013013 | PAYMENT RECEIVED--THANK YOU | | 450.00 |
| 01/18 | 01/20 | 24036215019664 | Real Music | Clover, IL | 115.50 |
| 02/02 | 02/03 | 242753050337531 | Books 'n' News | Montclair, MO | 13.90 |
| 02/01 | 02/03 | 242753950329000 | Nick's Candy | Montclair, MO | 4.60 |

| DAYS IN BILLING PERIOD: 25 | | Purchases | Cash Advance |
|---|---|---|---|
| **Balance Subject to Interest Charge** | > | 85.07% | .00 |
| **ANNUAL PERCENTAGE RATE** | > | 16.00% | 27.00% |

| 2012 Totals Year-to-Date | |
|---|---|
| **Total fees charged in 20XX** | $0.00 |
| **Total interest charged in 20XX** | $1.13 |

## Concept Application

Opening a credit card account is one way to start building your credit history. Most credit card applications can be completed online. When completing a credit card application, you must provide the following: your name, social security number, address, how long you have lived at that address, any previous addresses, whether you own or rent your home, your date of birth, your marital status, your gross (pre-tax) annual income(s), the name of your employer, and length of employment. Credit card companies will then use this information and research your credit history to create a credit profile.

Credit card companies want to know what types of credit you use, and how much credit you have used, the length of time your accounts have been open, and whether you paid your bills on time. Two of the most important factors that credit card companies consider are timeliness of payments and the amount of debt you have compared to your credit limit. If you have paid a bill late even once, that will be noted. If you already have a credit card, and your credit limit is $5,000 with a balance of $4,889.32, your application for a second credit card might be denied. If this is your first credit card, remember that paying your bills on time and carrying a low monthly balance on your credit accounts is critical to establishing a good credit history for the rest of your life.



### Critical Thinking

1. What is the default Annual Percentage Rate (APR) in the Schumer box on page 60? What mightcause the APR to default to a higher percentage? Why is a high APR bad?

2. What other fees do you need to be aware of before you accept the terms of any credit card?

3. Why is it critical to review the terms in the Schumer box before applying for a credit card?

| Bank Disclosures | |
|---|---|
| Annual Percentage Rate (APR) for purchases | 11.99% variable. |
| Other APRs | Balance transfer APR: As long as first balance transfer is completed within 9 months from date of account opening, 0.00% for 9 months from date of first balance transfer. After that, 11.99% variable.<br>Cash advance APR: 20.99% variable.<br>Default APR: 29.99% variable. See explanation below.* |
| Variable rate information | Your APRs may vary each billing period. **<br>The purchase and balance transfer APR equals the Prime Rate plus 5.99%. The cash advance APR equals the Prime Rate plus 14.99% (never lower than 19.99%).<br>The default APR equals the U.S. Prime Rate plus up to 23.99%. |
| Grace period for repayment of the balance for purchases | At least 20 days if you pay the total balance in full by the due date every billing period. If you do not, you will not get a grace period. |
| Method of computing the balance for purchases | Average daily balance. This includes new purchases. |
| Minimum finance charge | 50 cents. |
| Annual fees | None. |
| Fee for purchases made in a foreign currency | 3% of each purchase after it is converted into US dollars. |
| Other fees | Balance transfer fee: 3% of each balance transfer; $5 minimum. There is no fee with the 0.00% APR balance transfer offer described above. Cash advance fee: 3% of each cash advance; $5 minimum.<br>Late fee: $15 on balances up to $100<br>$29 on balances of $100 up to $250<br>$39 on balances of $250 and over<br>Over-the-credit-line fee:$35 |

* How can your actions trigger the default APR? If you default under any card agreement you have with us because you

1) do not make the minimum payment when due,

2) go over the credit line, or

3) make a payment to us that is not honored,

all your APRs may automatically increase to the default APR. We set your default APR by reviewing (1) the seriousness of your default with us and (2) your credit history.

** How do we calculate variable rates? For each billing period we use the Prime Rate published in The Wall Street Journal two business days before the Statement/Closing Date.

How do we apply your payments? We apply your payments to low APR balances first. You cannot pay off higher APR balances until you pay off lower APR balances. That means your savings from any promotional APR offer will be reduced if you make purchases or cash advances that have higher APRs.

Rates, fees, and terms may change: We have the right to change the rates, fees, and terms at any time, for any reason, in accordance with the cardmember agreement and applicable law. These reasons may be based on information in your credit report, such as your failure to make payments to another creditor when due, amounts owed to other creditors, the number of credit accounts outstanding, or the number of credit inquiries. These reasons may also include competitive or market-related factors. If we make a change for any of these reasons, you will receive advance notice and a right to opt out in accordance with applicable law.

Signature ______________________ Date ______________

# Activity: Loans

**AS YOU READ,** learn the vocabulary. **AFTER YOU READ,** check your understanding through Fact and Idea Review, Critical Thinking Questions, and an Extension Activity.

### Understanding Your Loan Options

Some day you will need to borrow money for a car, for school, or a house. It is important to understand your loan options. You should consider what type of loan you need for your situation and what you feel comfortable paying. As an informed consumer, always shop around with several lenders to compare loan options. If you provide basic financial information, such as income, assets, and debt, lenders can provide you with a rate.

Most loans are structured with a set number of payments scheduled for a set time frame, which can be anywhere from three months to 30 years; these are installment loans. A mortgage is a type of installment loan.

Home loans are closed-end installment loans, and the home itself serves as security for the loan. Closed-end means you cannot change the number or amount of payments, the loan's maturity date, or other terms. One kind of mortgage loan requires an oversized payment due at the end of the life of the loan, hence the name **balloon payment**. It can be a shock to your finances to have to pay $1,000 for your last payment when you were paying $100 a month. These kinds of loans are more common in commercial real estate.

Once you have been approved for a loan and you pledge your home as security for the loan, you have the right to cancel the loan in writing within three business days of signing it. This is called your **right of rescission**, provided by the Truth in Lending Act of 1968 to promote accurate disclosures about the loan.

When shopping for loans you will be offered many options. One option for the loan is buying different points. Points are fees you are willing to pay in order to get a lower interest rate. The number of points refers to the percentage of the loan amount that you pay. For example, "2 points" means a charge of 2 percent of the loan amount. You will need to consider the immediate cost of points and the long-term benefits of a lower interest rate to decide if buying points is the best option for you. You should research and carefully consider all options presented to you during the loan application process to make sure you get the best loan for your needs. Some other loan types include:

- Home improvement loans are closed-end installment loans. Home equity loans can be closed-end or open-end loans.
- Vehicle loans are closed-end installment loans and can be use for new or used vehicles.
- A personal line of credit is an open-end loan with a preset limit.

- Student loans cover the cost of technical training, college, or post-secondary school. You generally do not have to start paying student loans back until six to twelve months after you leave school. These loans often have flexible repayment schedules.

Take your time while loan shopping and compare offers from many lenders to get the best deal for you.

## Vocabulary

**Balloon payment** a final loan payment that is much larger than the other installments.

**Right of rescission** a right provided by the Truth in Lending Act, that gives borrowers up to three business days to cancel a loan or other credit transaction for which their home is pledged as security.

## Fact and Idea Review

1. How do student loans differ from personal loans?

2. How does a balloon loan differ from an installment loan?

## Critical Thinking

1. Why is it important to compare loans and get offers from several lenders? What might happen if a person accepts the first offer they receive?

2. How is researching loans, lenders, and loan options a critical part of managing your finances and meeting your financial goals? Explain and provide examples.

3. Research various loan options and describe each one. For example, mortgage points are one option to lower your interest rate. Why is it important to know all your options before selecting a loan?

______________________________________________

______________________________________________

______________________________________________

______________________________________________

**Extension Activity**

Some day you will need to borrow money. Research loan rates online to see what kind of interest rates and terms are available for a new or used vehicle loan, a 30-year fixed home loan, or a student loan. Create a table or spreadsheet to present your findings along with an explanation of what you learned.

# Activity: Debt

**AS YOU READ,** learn the vocabulary. **AS YOU READ,** check your understanding through Fact and Idea Review, Critical Thinking Questions, and an Extension Activity.

### Managing Debt

Debt can be caused by overspending, job loss, illness, family issues, poor money management, or other issues. Spiraling debt can be overwhelming, as high balances, late fees, and interest rates pile up. Debt can cause serious stress and serious damage to your **credit history.** Saving money or reaching your financial goals is impossible when your money is going to pay down debt. In some cases, filing **bankruptcy** is the last resort for people to reorganize their finances.

However, you can climb out of debt. Most creditors will work to try to keep your payments affordable. You should stop using your credit cards immediately so as not to increase your debt. Your number one priority should be to pay down your debt. Debt credit counselors can help by combining all your debt into one loan with manageable payments. This way you only have to pay one loan instead of paying several different creditors at several different interest rates.

You can avoid debt in the first place by maintaining good credit. Credit scores range from 300 to 850. In general, the higher the debt load, the lower your score; the lower the debt load, the higher your score. This is one aspect of your score. Good credit is established when you enter into an agreement with a lender and pay the money back as agreed or sooner.

Having a good or excellent **credit rating** can benefit you in many ways. Good credit qualifies you for credit cards with lower interest rates, higher credit limits, more rewards, and lower fees; basically you are getting more money at a lower cost. Car, home, and personal loans also give lower interest rates to individuals who have good credit, which means lower monthly payments. Your insurance rates might also decrease. You will be rewarded for maintaining good credit.

Many jobs will check your credit history to see how you manage your finances. Government jobs may require a security clearance, and people with poor credit will not be given clearance for the job. Financial jobs also require that employees have good credit.

Paying yourself first is a useful strategy for meeting your financial goals. The Pareto Principle, or 10-10-80 rule, is a simple concept that sets aside 10 percent of your money for savings, 10 percent for charity, and 80 percent to living expenses. This works well if your income is steady. Another similar concept with different percentage splits is the 10-10-10-70, rule which states you should save 10 percent, invest 10 percent, give 10 percent, and live off the remaining 70 percent. Both of these plans have a saving and spending aspect, which is the basis of any budget.

To avoid debt and maintain good credit as an individual or as a family, the same rules apply. It is critical to set goals, establish a budget, and stick to your budget. You must be disciplined, have self control, and have a willingness to live within your means.

## Vocabulary

**Credit rating** an evaluation of a consumer's credit history

**Credit history** a pattern of past behavior in regard to repaying debt

**Bankruptcy** legal relief from repaying certain debts

## Fact and Idea Review

1. What are the 10-10-80 and 10-10-10-70 rules?

2. How can a good or excellent credit rating benefit you?

## Critical Thinking

1. What can you do to address credit and debt issues?

2. What skills are necessary to address credit and debt issues?

3. Why do you think people fall into the credit card trap so easily?

## Extension Activity

Consider what you need to do to establish and maintain good credit. What are your personal and family goals in relation to credit and debt? Create a table or spreadsheet to illustrate the steps needed to meet your goals and maintain your credit.

Name ______________________ Date ____________ Period ________

# Consumer Credit Usage Patterns

20 YOUR PERSONAL FINANCIAL PLAN

**Purpose:** To create a record of current consumer debt balances.

**Financial Planning Activities:** Record account names, numbers, and payments for current consumer debts.

**Suggested websites:** www.ftc.gov, www.creditcards.com, Lemon Wallet

## Automobile, Education, Personal, and Installment Loans

| Financial institution | Account number | Current balance | Monthly payment |
|---|---|---|---|
| | | | |
| | | | |
| | | | |
| | | | |
| | | | |

## Charge Accounts and Credit Cards

| Financial institution | Account number | Current balance | Monthly payment |
|---|---|---|---|
| | | | |
| | | | |
| | | | |
| | | | |
| | | | |

## Other Loans (overdraft protection, home equity, life insurance loan)

| Financial institution | Account number | Current balance | Monthly payment |
|---|---|---|---|
| | | | |
| | | | |
| | | | |
| | | | |
| | | | |

**Totals** ____________ ____________

$$\text{Debt payments-to-income ratio} = \frac{\text{Total monthly payments}}{\text{Net (after-tax) income}}$$

## What's Next for Your Personal Financial Plan?

- Survey three or four individuals to determine their uses of credit.
- Talk to several people to learn how they first established credit.

Name ______________________ Date ____________ Period ________

# Credit Card/Charge Account Comparison

**Purpose:** To compare the benefits and costs associated with different credit cards and charge accounts.

**Financial Planning Activities:** Analyze advertisements and credit card application forms and contract various financial institutions to obtain the information requested below.

**Suggested Websites:** www.bankrate.com, www.creditcards.com, www.consumerfinance.gov

| | | | |
|---|---|---|---|
| Type of credit/charge account | | | |
| Name of company/account | | | |
| Address/phone | | | |
| Website | | | |
| Type of purchases that can be made | | | |
| Annual fee (if any) | | | |
| Annual percentage rate (APR) (interest calculation information) | | | |
| Credit limit for new customers | | | |
| Minimum monthly payment | | | |
| **Other costs:**<br>- Credit report<br>- late fee<br>- other ________ | | | |
| Restrictions (age, minimum annual income) | | | |
| Other information for consumers to consider | | | |
| Frequent flyer or other bonus points | | | |

## What's Next for Your Personal Financial Plan?

- Make a list of the pros and cons of using credit cards or charge accounts.
- Contact a local credit bureau to obtain information on the services provided and the fees charged.

Name ______________________ Date ____________ Period ________

# Consumer Loan Comparison



**Purpose:** To compare the costs associated with different sources of loans.

**Financial Planning Activities:** Contact or visit a bank, a credit union, and a consumer finance company to obtain information on a loan for a specific purpose.

**Suggested Websites:** www.eloan.com, www.wellsfargo.com, www.ftc.gov

| **Type of financial institution** | | | |
|---|---|---|---|
| Name | | | |
| Address | | | |
| Phone | | | |
| Website | | | |
| What collateral is required? | | | |
| Amount of down payment | | | |
| Length of loan (months) | | | |
| Amount of monthly payments | | | |
| Total amount to be repaid (monthly amount × number of months + down payment) | | | |
| Total finance charge/cost of credit | | | |
| Annual percentage rate (APR) | | | |
| **Other costs**<br>- credit life insurance<br>- credit report<br>- other ____________ | | | |
| Is a cosigner required? | | | |
| Other information | | | |

## What's Next for Your Personal Financial Plan?

- Ask several individuals how they would compare loans at different financial institutions.
- Survey several friends or relatives to determine if they ever cosigned for a loan. If yes, what were the consequences of cosigning?

# 7 Spending: Wise Buying of Motor Vehicles

## Activity: Your Personal Finances

**AS YOU READ**, learn the vocabulary. **AFTER YOU READ**, check your understanding through Fact and Idea Review, Critical Thinking Questions, and an Extension Activity.

### Factors that Impact Your Budget

**Fuel Economy** In 1975, two years after a severe shortage of oil in the United States, the U.S. Congress enacted regulations to improve the average fuel efficiency of cars and trucks and to help conserve energy. In 1978, these Corporate Average Fuel Economy standards, called CAFE standards required passenger cars to get a minimum of 18 miles per gallon (mpg). In 2010, passenger cars were required to get at least 27.5 mpg, and by 2030 the minimum requirement will be 52 mpg. Automakers that do not meet the CAFE standards must pay a penalty.

**Health Insurance** In 2010, the Patient Protection and Affordable Care Act was passed. One of the provisions of this act lets young adults remain on their parents' health plans until the age of 26. For a young person in school or entering the workforce, this can save money.

These types of public policies directly impact your personal financial decisions. When prices at the gas pump are high, consumers will drive less and purchase more fuel-efficient cars. This is good for the environment and for consumers' wallets. For a person in his or her early to mid-twenties, he or she may be able to go to college or find a job without the stress of finding cost-effective health insurance.

**Your Budget** The kinds of personal financial decisions you make is something that employers consider, too. By making good personal financial decisions you demonstrate that you can be trusted to do the same for your employer. When you set your long- and short-term financial goals, prioritize them, plan how you can budget and save to fulfill them, and balance your resources, you are establishing the kind of skills employers want.

Not making good financial decisions can negatively affect your future. Checking your personal financial history is a requirement for some jobs. An employer may refuse employment to someone with a bad financial history, even if the person is capable of doing the job well.

Say you are offered a job with a higher wage than your last job. If you have been tracking your budget and expenses, then you will know how much of a **budget surplus** you will have to set aside for a special purchase or to set aside for savings. A **budget deficit**, on the other hand, should be a wake-up call to reorganize your finances. Reviewing your financial goals, reducing your spending, and sticking to your budget can help you improve your financial situation. Making good personal financial decisions will positively affect your future.

## Vocabulary

**Budget surplus** an amount by which revenue exceeds spending

**Budget deficit** an amount by which spending exceeds revenue

## Fact and Idea Review

1. What are some examples of public policy issues that impact personal financial decisions?

2. What financial skills might an employer want you to have?

## Critical Thinking

1. Explain how public policy issues might impact your budget and financial decisions.

2. Why is it important to set financial goals and create a personal budget?

3. Why would good personal financial skills appeal to an employer?

## Extension Activity

Create a personal budget. Make a list identifying your financial goals, and then narrow that list to three primary goals. Be sure you estimate your income and expenses realistically and then balance the two for your budget. Do you have a surplus or deficit? Will you be able to achieve your goals with your current budget? What changes can you make to your budget to achieve your goals?

## Activity: Needs, Wants, and Values

**AS YOU READ,** learn the vocabulary. **AFTER YOU READ,** check your understanding through Fact and Idea Review, Critical Thinking Questions, and an Extension Activity.

### Managing Your Purchases

If you are a well-organized person who makes lists and allots time for grocery shopping and cooking, you are likely to save more money. If you do not plan meals or make time to shop, and tend to eat out frequently, then you are likely to spend more money. Time, and how you utilize your time, influences what you purchase.

Resources also influence what you eat. How much money you and your family have will determine what you purchase. Being a knowledgeable consumer will also impact what you buy. If you are a good cook or you're creative with ingredients, you can buy in bulk and make recipes from scratch rather than buying processed **convenience foods.**

In addition, food choices can be influenced by personal preferences and outside factors. Think of some of your favorite foods. Why do you like them? Factors such as family, culture, religion, region, friends, and the media can impact what choices you make as a consumer.

Your choices can also be impacted by personal factors. What you purchase says something about you. Every time you purchase meat, vegetables, or fruit at the grocery store you are indicating something about your needs, wants, and values. What types of food does your family need to eat? What kinds of food does your family want to eat? Remember, needs and wants can be different things.

How do your values impact the food you buy? For example, do you only buy locally grown, in-season produce and grass-fed meats or do you buy whatever is on sale? Do you read the **Daily Values** on food labels to maximize the nutrients you are eating? Or do you compare the **unit price** to find the best deal? These are the sorts of questions you answer with each purchase.

In addition to food, another purchases your family makes based on need and personal values is gasoline. For some people, the environment is a priority so they will try to reduce their fuel consumption. These people might drive fuel efficient cars, hybrids, carpool, use public transportation, bike, or walk to the store or the office. Others may try to conserve fuel because the high price of gasoline cuts into their budget, and any benefit to the environment is secondary.

By being aware of what you are purchasing and why, you are taking a step toward being a responsible consumer and using your resources wisely.

## Vocabulary

**Daily values** nutrient reference amounts set by the U.S. Food and Drug Administration for use on food labels

**Unit price** the cost per unit of measurement

**Convenience foods** foods processed in ways that make them easier to consume

## Fact and Idea Reviews

1. What is the difference between a need and a want?

2. What is an example of making a purchase based on a personal value?

## Critical Thinking

1. What factors influence purchases? Explain.

2. What is the relationship between the environment and consumer resources?

3. Why is it important to take responsibility for personal and family financial decisions based on needs, wants, and values?

## Extension Activity

It is important to take responsibility for your financial decisions. Make a list identifying your needs, wants, and values, then make another list identifying your family's needs, wants and values. What financial decisions have you and your family made that were based on one or more of these factors? How might your needs, wants, and values influence your future financial decisions? Summarize your conclusions.

Name ________________ Date ________ Period ________

# Consumer Purchase Comparison

**Purpose:** To research and evaluate brands and store services for a major consumer purchase.

**Financial Planning Activities:** When considering the purchase of a major consumer item, use advertisements, catalogs, an online search, store visits, and other sources to obtain the information below.

**Suggested Websites & Apps:** www.consumerreports.org, www.consumerworld.org, www.clarkhoward.com

23 YOUR PERSONAL FINANCIAL PLAN



**Product**

Exact description (size, model, features, etc.)

Conduct online research to obtain information and buying suggestions regarding the product.

Source ________________ Source ________________

Date ________________ Date ________________

What buying suggestions are presented in the articles?

Which brands are recommended in these articles? Why?

Contact or visit two or three stores or online retailers that sell the product you want to obtain the following information:

| | Buying Location 1 | Buying Location 2 | Buying Location 3 |
|---|---|---|---|
| Business name | | | |
| Address (if applicable) | | | |
| Phone/website | | | |
| Brand name/cost | | | |
| Variation from the description above (if any) | | | |
| Warranty (describe) | | | |

Which brand would you prefer to buy? At which store would you buy this product? Why?

## What's Next for Your Personal Financial Plan?

- Which consumer information sources are most valuable for your future buying decisions?
- List guidelines to use in the future when making major purchases.

Name ____________ Date ________ Period ________

# Used Car Purchase Comparison

**Purpose:** To research and evaluate different types and sources of used vehicles.

**Financial Planning Activities:** When considering a used car purchase, use advertisements, online sources, and visits to new and used car dealers to obtain the information below.

**Suggested Websites & Apps:** www.carburingtips.com, www.kbb.com, www.safercar.gov

| **Automobile** (year, make, model) | | | |
|---|---|---|---|
| Dealership name/online source | | | |
| Address | | | |
| Phone | | | |
| Website/email | | | |
| Cost | | | |
| Mileage | | | |
| Condition of vehicle | | | |
| Condition of tires | | | |
| Audio system | | | |
| Other options | | | |
| Warranty (if applicable) | | | |
| Inspection items: - Rust, major dents? | | | |
| - Oil or fluid leaks? | | | |
| - Condition of brakes? | | | |
| - Proper operation of heater, wipers, other accessories? | | | |
| - Other information | | | |

## What's Next for Your Personal Financial Plan?

- Maintain a record of automobile operating costs.
- Prepare a plan for regular maintenance of your vehicle.

24 YOUR PERSONAL FINANCIAL PLAN

Name ________________ Date ________ Period ________

# Buying versus Leasing a Vehicle

**Purpose:** To compare the costs of buying or leasing an automobile or other vehicle.

**Financial Planning Activities:** Obtain costs related to leasing and buying a vehicle.

**Suggested Websites & Apps:** www.leaseesource.com, www.moneyunder30.com/buy-vs-lease-calculator, Rodo

### Purchase Costs

Total vehicle cost, including sales tax ($________)

Down payment (or full amount if paying cash) $________

Monthly loan payment: $________ times ________ month loan (This item is zero if the vehicle is not financed.) $________

Opportunity cost of down payment (or total cost of the vehicle if bought for cash):

$________ number of years of financing/ownership times ________ percent (interest rate that funds could earn) $________

**Less:** estimated value of vehicle at end of loan term/ownership $________

**Total cost to buy**........................................ $________

### Leasing Costs

Security Deposit $________

Monthly lease payments: $________ times ________ months $________

Opportunity cost of security deposit: $________ times years time ________ percent

$________

End-of-lease charges (if applicable) * $________

**Total cost to lease**........................................ $________

** With a closed-end lease, charges for extra mileage or excessive wear and tear; with an open-end lease, end-of-lease payment if appraised value is less than estimated ending value.*

## What's Next for Your Personal Financial Plan?

- Prepare a list of future actions to use when buying, financing, and leasing a car.
- Maintain a record of operating costs and maintenance actions for your vehicle.

Name ______________________ Date ____________ Period ________

# Legal Services Cost Comparison

**Purpose:** To compare the costs of services from different sources of legal assistance.

**Financial Planning Activities:** Contact various legal service providers (lawyers, prepaid legal services, legal aid society) and online sources to compare costs and available services.

**Suggested Websites & Apps:** www.nolo.com, www.americanbar.org, Ask a Lawyer



| **Type of legal service** | | | |
|---|---|---|---|
| Organization name | | | |
| Address | | | |
| Phone | | | |
| Website/email | | | |
| Contact person | | | |
| Recommended by | | | |
| Areas of specialization | | | |
| Cost of initial consultation | | | |
| Cost of simple will | | | |
| Cost method for other services – flat fee, hourly rate, or contingency basis | | | |
| Other information | | | |

## What's Next for Your Personal Financial Plan?

- Determine the best option for your future legal needs.
- Maintain a file of legal documents and other financial records.

# 8 Spending: Planning Your Housing

## How Do People Choose?

Learning Objective: learn about the other side of shopping for a home.

There are a number of surprising things that are known to influence the sale of a home. For example, if the home smells like freshly-baked cookies, the attractiveness of your real estate agent, etc., can sway a buyer's decision. For this assignment, you are going to be taking the role of a home "stager."

1. If you were shopping for a home, list the five most important things you would look for when touring a potential house:

    1. ______________________________
    2. ______________________________
    3. ______________________________
    4. ______________________________
    5. ______________________________

2. As a stager, you realize that the living room in the house you are staging has real wood paneling, olive green walls, ceiling tiles, and bright orange shag carpet (over the hardwood floors). Using specifics, what suggestions would you make to get this home ready to sell?

______________________________

______________________________

______________________________

______________________________

______________________________

______________________________

______________________________

______________________________

______________________________

______________________________

3. Explain the role smell plays in the home buying decision. Do you think that this is an important part of staging a house?

4. How does having unfinished space affect your ability to sell a house?

5. List 10 things you might do to help a house sell faster.

6. Research the most popular wall paint colors, cabinet colors, and carpet or flooring options, and list what you find below.

7. How much money do you think should be invested in getting a house ready to sell? What should be considered when making this type of budget?

# Buying a House

Learning Objective: see the importance of someone's financial constraints when selecting a house.

1. The Tremblays have been pre-approved by their bank to enter the housing market with a mortgage interest rate of 8.6 percent. They have $30,000 set aside for a down payment. They have also calculated that they can afford a monthly payment of $1,350. The Tremblays have narrowed their search to three houses and are hoping their financial constraints won't narrow their choices. The three houses cost the following amounts: $150,000, $270,000, and $400,000. The bank will add $50 to each mortgage payment if they put less than 20 percent down and an additional fee of $50 more to each payment if they put less than 10 percent down.

   a. Which of these houses can the Tremblays afford with a 30-year mortgage?

   b. Which of these houses can they afford with a 15-year mortgage?

   c. Which house do you think the Tremblays should buy? Exlain your reasoning.

2. The Young household is looking at buying a house. The three houses they are looking at cost the following: $160,000, $190,000 and $210,000. They can pay up to $900 in monthly mortgage payments. The Youngs currently have $18,000 set aside for a down payment. Similar to the Tremblays' bank, the Youngs' bank will add $40 to each mortgage payment if they put less than 20 percent down and an additional fee of $30 more to each payment if they put less than 10 percent down.

a. Which of these houses can the Youngs afford with a 30-year mortgage at an interest rate of 3.5 percent?

b. Which of these houses can they afford with a 15-year mortgage at an interest rate of 2.8 percent?

c. Which house do you think the Youngs should buy? Explain your reasoning.

3. Private mortgage insurance, or PMI (which is similar to the extra fees shown above), can greatly affect the affordability of housing. This payment is normally made until you meet a certain threshold of mortgage payments. Suppose the Anderson family bought a house with zero down as part of their mortgage agreement; they have to pay an extra $75 per month in PMI until they have paid off 20 percent of the principal balance on their home. They bought a $180,000 house on a 30-year mortgage at an interest rate of 13 percent. Using this information, their monthly payment would be $1,991.16 without the extra fee.

a. How long will it take the Andersons to pay off the first 20 percent of their house?

**b.** How much will they have paid in PMI fees in this time?

**c.** How much interest will the Andersons end up paying over the life of this loan?

**d.** What is the total amount the Andersons paid for their $180,000 home?

**4.** Many developed countries require a 20 percent down payment in order to purchase a home (counterintuitively, many of these countries have higher home ownership that the USA, which does not have this requirement). How do you think individuals and the housing market in the USA would be affected if the 20 percent down payment requirement was passed as a law?

Name ______________________ Date ____________ Class ________

## Renting versus Buying Housing

**Purpose:** To compare the cost of renting or buying your place of residence.

**Financial Planning Activities:** Obtain estimates for comparable housing units for the data requested below.

**Suggested Websites & Apps:** www.homefair.com, www.nerdwallet.com/mortgages/rent-vs-buy-calculator, Realtor

### Rental Costs

| | |
|---|---|
| Annual rent payments (monthly rent $________ × 12) | $________ |
| Renter's insurance | $________ |
| Interest lost on security deposit (deposit times after-tax savings account interest rate) | $________ |
| **Total annual cost of renting** | $________ |

### Buying Costs

| | |
|---|---|
| Annual mortgage payments (monthly mortgage payment $________ × 12) | $________ |
| Property taxes (annual costs) | $________ |
| Homeowner's insurance (annual premium) | $________ |
| Estimated maintenance and repairs | $________ |
| After-tax interest lost because of down payment/closing costs | $________ |
| **Less:** financial benefits of home ownership | $________ |
| Growth in equity | $–________ |
| Tax savings for property taxes (annual mortgage interest time tax rate) | $–________ |
| **Total annual cost of buying** | $________ |

## What's Next for Your Personal Financial Plan?

- Determine if renting or buying is the best option for you at the current time.
- List some circumstances or actions that might change your housing needs.

Name ______ Date ______ Class ______

# Apartment Rental Comparison

**Purpose:** To evaluate and compare rental housing options.

**Financial Planning Activities:** Obtain the information requested below to compare costs and facilities of three apartments.

**Suggested Websites & Apps:** www.apartments.com, www.apartmentguide.com, www.thespruce.com/apartment-living-4127933, Zillow Rentals, Trulia Rentals



| Name of rental company or person | Apartment 1 | Apartment 2 | Apartment 3 |
|---|---|---|---|
| Address | | | |
| Phone/e-mail | | | |
| Monthly rent | | | |
| Amount of security deposit | | | |
| Length of lease | | | |
| Utilities included in rent | | | |
| Parking facilities | | | |
| Storage area in building | | | |
| Laundry facilities | | | |
| Distance to schools | | | |
| Distance to public transportation | | | |
| Distance to shopping | | | |
| Poll, recreation area, other facilities | | | |
| Estimated utility costs:<br>- Electric<br>- Cable/internet<br>- Gas<br>- Water | | | |
| Other costs | | | |
| Other information | | | |

## What's Next for Your Personal Financial Plan?

- Which of these rental units would best serve your current housing needs?
- What additional information should be considered when renting an apartment?

Name ______________ Date ______________ Class ______________



# Housing Affordability and Mortgage Qualification

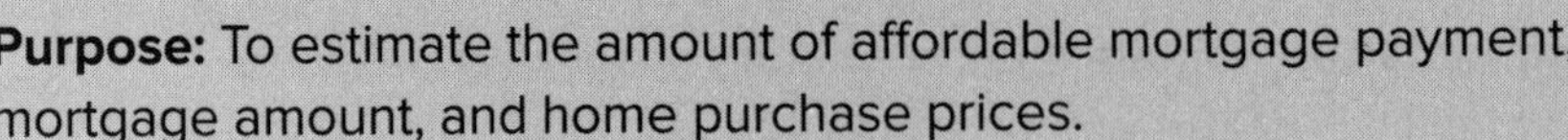

**Purpose:** To estimate the amount of affordable mortgage payment, mortgage amount, and home purchase prices.

**Financial Planning Activities:** Enter the amounts requested to estimate the amount of affordable mortgage payment, mortgage amount, and home purchase price.

**Suggested Websites & Apps:** www.mba.org, Mortgage Calculator, Mortgage by Zillow

**Step 1**

Determine your monthly gross income (annual income divided by 12) $______________

**Step 2**

With a down payment of at least 10 percent, lenders use 28 percent of monthly gross income as a guideline for TIPI (taxes, insurance, principal, and interest), 36 percent of monthly gross income as a guideline for TIPI plus other debt payments (enter 0.28 or 0.36). ×______________

**Step 3**

Subtract other debt payments (such as payments on an auto loan), if applicable. −______________

Subtract estimated monthly costs of property taxes and homeowner's insurance. −______________

**Affordable monthly mortgage payment** .......................... $______________

**Step 4**

Divide this amount by the monthly mortgage payment per $1,000 based on current mortgage rates (see Exhibit 8-7). For example, for an 8 percent, 30-year loan, the number would be $7.34. ÷______________

Multiply by $1,000. ×______________

**Step 5**

Divide your affordable mortgage amount by 1 minus the fractional portion of your down payment (for example, 0.9 for a 10 percent down payment). (division symbol) ______________

**Affordable home purchase price** .......................... $______________

**Affordable mortgage amount** $______________

***Note:*** The two ratios used by lending institutions (Step 2) and other loan requirements are likely to vary based on a variety of factors, including the type of mortgage, the amount of the down payment, your income level, your credit score, and current interest rates. If you have other debts, lenders will calculate both ratios and then use the one that allows you greater flexibility in borrowing.

## What's Next for Your Personal Financial Plan?

- Identify actions you might need to take to qualify for a mortgage.
- Discuss your mortgage qualifications with a mortgage broker or other lender.

Name ______________________ Date ____________ Class ________

# Mortgage Company Comparison

**Purpose:** To compare the services and costs for different home mortgage options.

**Financial Planning Activities:** Using online research and other sources, obtain the information requested below to compare the services and costs for different home mortgage companies.

**Suggested Websites:** www.hsh.com, www.eloan.com, www.bankrate.com, Bankrate Mortgages, Rocket Mortgage

| Amount of mortgage: $________ | Down Payment $________ | Years: ________ |
|---|---|---|
| Company | | |
| Address | | |
| Phone | | |
| Website | | |
| Contact person/e-mail | | |
| Application, credit report, and property appraisal fees | | |
| Loan origination fee | | |
| Other fees, charges (commitment, title, tax transfer) | | |
| **Fixed-rate mortgage** | | |
| Monthly payment | | |
| Discount points | | |
| **Adjustable-rate mortgage** | | |
| • Time until first rate charge | | |
| • Frequency of rate charge | | |
| Payment cap | | |
| Interest rate cap | | |
| Rate index used | | |
| Commitment period | | |
| Other information | | |

## What's Next for Your Personal Financial Plan?

- What additional information should be considered when selecting a mortgage?
- Which of these mortgage companies would best serve your current and future needs?

# 9 Managing Risk: Home and Auto Insurance

## Insurance

**AS YOU READ,** learn the vocabulary. **AFTER YOU READ,** check your understanding through Fact and Idea Review, Critical Thinking Questions, and an Extension Activity.

### Risk Management

Having **insurance** protection as a part of your financial planning will minimize financial losses from accidents. Some types of insurance include homeowner's, health, and life.

Homeowner's insurance protects property from fires, theft, or damage from weather. It provides coverage for damages to the home or loss of contents belonging to the homeowner. Homeowners insurance also provides liability coverage for accidents that may occur at the home. For example, if someone falls off a ladder while working on your roof, your home insurance will pay for his or her hospital bill. The standard amount for liability coverage is around $300,000. Insurance companies have two ways to compensate you for your losses. They can provide you with the actual cash value of the lost items, or they can replace the items with comparable new ones. The replacement coverage is more expensive.

Another important type of insurance is health insurance. Medical costs can overwhelm those who do not have coverage. Coverage for hospital stays, routine doctor visits, and prescription drugs are minimum requirements. Major medical coverage is for major illnesses when longer hospital stays, treatments, and medications are required. Most people are insured through their employer, although a self-employed person can obtain individual health insurance policies. Plans generally fall under two categories; fee-for-service or managed care plans.

A fee-for-service plan allows you to have your choice of doctors and hospitals. You must keep good records of your paperwork. You are charged for each medical service and your insurance pays a portion of that fee. Fee-for-service plans have a yearly deductible such as $500 for an individual and $1,000 for a family. Generally, the insurance company will pay 80 percent and you will have to pay the remaining 20 percent after you have paid your deductible. Fee-for-service plans cost a little more for the freedom to choose doctors and hospitals.

Managed care plans can vary, but they are similar in that they involve a network of selected doctors and hospitals who agree to provide care for predetermined fees. Managed car plans emphasize preventive care. Managed care plans require a **co-payment** to be paid by the patient to the doctor or hospital for every visit. Co-payments vary but are generally around $20 for a doctor visit and $100 for an emergency room visit.

Life insurance should also be a part of your financial plan. When someone dies, his or her life insurance will provide money to their dependents. How much life insurance you need is correlated to how many people depend on you for financial support. Someone who is married with children would need more life insurance coverage than someone who is 25 and single. The cost of life insurance is based on your age, gender, health, your family's health history, your occupation, and your recreational activities. To qualify for life insurance, you are required to fill out a form that details your health history, age, and other factors.

## Vocabulary

**Insurance** purchased protection that guarantees to pay you in the event of certain specified losses

**Co-payment** a flat fee given to a health care provider at the time of service

**Liability** legal responsibility to compensate someone who has suffered an injury or loss caused by another

## Fact and Idea Review

1. What is liability insurance? What is homeowner's insurance?

2. What is health insurance? What is life insurance?

## Critical Thinking

1. Why is it important to have property insurance and liability insurance as a part of individual and family financial plans?

2. Why is it important to have health insurance and life insurance as part of individual and family financial plans?

3. Which type of insurance would be most important for you to have now and in the future? Explain your choices.

**Extension Activity**

Select one type of insurance from the article. Research consumer options for this insurance type. What information is needed to apply? What factors influence costs? What options or choices do you have for the policy, and which would you choose? Where can you buy this insurance? What company would you select as your provider and seller? Summarize your findings.

Name ____________ Date ________ Period ______

# Current Insurance Policies and Needs

**Purpose:** To establish a record of current and needed insurance coverage.

**Financial Planning Activities:** List current insurance policies and areas where new or additional coverage is needed.

**Suggested Websites & Apps:** www.insure.com, www.accuquote.com



| Current Coverage | Needed Coverage |
|---|---|
| **Property Insurance** | |
| Company | |
| Policy no. | |
| Coverage amounts | |
| Deductible | |
| Annual premium | |
| Agent | |
| Address | |
| Phone | |
| Website | |

| Current Coverage | Needed Coverage |
|---|---|
| **Automobile Insurance** | |
| Company | |
| Policy no. | |
| Coverage amounts | |
| Deductible | |
| Annual premium | |
| Agent | |
| Address | |
| Phone | |
| Website | |

| Current Coverage | Needed Coverage |
|---|---|
| **Disability Income Insurance** | |
| Company | |
| Policy no. | |
| Coverage amounts | |
| Deductible | |
| Annual premium | |
| Agent | |
| Address | |
| Phone | |
| Website | |

| **Current Coverage** | **Needed Coverage** |
|---|---|
| **Health Insurance** | |
| Company | |
| Policy no. | |
| Coverage amounts | |
| Deductible | |
| Annual premium | |
| Agent | |
| Address | |
| Phone | |
| Website | |

| **Current Coverage** | **Needed Coverage** |
|---|---|
| **Life Insurance** | |
| Company | |
| Policy no. | |
| Coverage amounts | |
| Deductible | |
| Annual premium | |
| Agent | |
| Address | |
| Phone | |
| Website | |

## What's Next for Your Personal Financial Plan?

- Talk with friends and relatives to determine the types of insurance coverage they have.
- Conduct a web search for various types of insurance for which you need additional information.

Name ______________________ Date ____________ Period ________

## Home Inventory

**Purpose:** To create a record of personal belongings for use when settling home insurance claims.

**Financial Planning Activities:** For each area of the home, list your possessions, including a description (model, serial number), cost, and date of acquisition. Also consider taking photographs and videos of your possessions.

**Suggested Websites & Apps:** www.money.com, www.ambest.com, Home Inventory

| **Item, Description** | **Cost** | **Date Acquired** |
|---|---|---|
| Attic | | |
| | | |
| | | |
| Bathroom | | |
| | | |
| | | |
| Bedrooms | | |
| | | |
| | | |
| Family room | | |
| | | |
| | | |
| Living room | | |
| | | |
| | | |
| Hallways | | |
| | | |
| | | |
| Kitchen | | |
| | | |
| | | |

Dining room

Basement

Garage

Other items

### What's Next for Your Personal Financial Plan?

- Determine common items that may be overlooked when preparing a home inventory.
- Talk to a local insurance agent to determine the areas of protection that many people tend to overlook.

Name ______ Date ______ Period ______

# Determining Needed Property Insurance

**Purpose:** To determine property insurance needed for a home or apartment.

**Financial Planning Activities:** Estimate the value of items and your needs for the categories below.

**Suggested Websites & Apps:** www.iii.org, www.quicken.com, www.naic.org

YOUR PERSONAL FINANCIAL PLAN 33

**Real Property (This section not applicable to renters)**

Current replacement value of home $______

**Personal Property**

Estimated value of appliances, furniture, clothing, and other household items (conduct an inventory) $______

Type of coverage for personal property (check one)

Actual cash value ☐

Replacement value ☐

Additional coverage for items with limits on standard personal property coverage such as jewelry, firearms, silverware, and photographic, electronic, and computer equipment.

| Item | Amount |
|---|---|
| | |
| | |
| | |

**Personal Liability**

Amount of additional personal liability coverage desired for possible personal injury claims. $______

**Specialized Coverages**

If appropriate, investigate flood or earthquake coverage excluded from home insurance policies. $______

***Note:*** Use *Your Personal Financial Plan "Apartment/Home Insurance Comparison"* to compare companies, coverages, and costs for apartment or homeinsurance.

## What's Next for Your Personal Financial Plan?

- Outline the steps involved in planning your home insurance needs.
- Outline special types of property and liability insurance such as personal computer insurance, trip cancellation insurance, and liability insurance.

YOUR PERSONAL FINANCIAL PLAN 34

Name ______________________ Date ____________ Period ________

# Apartment/Home Insurance Comparison

**Purpose:** To research and compare companies, coverages, and costs for apartment or home insurance.

**Financial Planning Activities:** Contract three insurance agents to obtain the information requested below.

**Suggested Websites & Apps:** www.freeinsurancequotes.com, www.insure.com, www.insureuonline.org

Type of building ☐ apartment ☐ home ☐ condominium

Location ______________________

Type of construction ____________ Age of building ____________

Insurance company name ______________________

Agent's name, address, and phone ______________________

| **Coverage** | **Premium** | **Premium** | **Premium** |
|---|---|---|---|
| Dwelling | | | |
| $ | | | |
| Other structure | | | |
| $ | | | |
| (does not apply to apartment/condo coverage) | | | |
| Personal property | | | |
| $ | | | |
| Additional living expenses | | | |
| $ | | | |
| Personal liability | | | |
| Bodily injury | | | |
| $ | | | |
| Property damage | | | |
| $ | | | |
| Medical payments | | | |
| Per person | | | |
| $ | | | |

Per accident

$

Deductible amount

Other coverage

$

Service charges or fees

**Total Premium**

**What's Next for Your Personal Financial Plan?**

- List the reasons most commonly given by renters for not having renter's insurance.
- Determine cost differences for home insurance among various local agents and online providers.

YOUR PERSONAL FINANCIAL PLAN 35

Name ______________________ Date ____________ Period ________

## Automobile Insurance Cost Comparison

**Purpose:** To research and compare companies, coverages, and costs for auto insurance.

**Financial Planning Activities:** Contact three insurance agents to obtain the information requested below.

**Suggested Websites & Apps:** www.autoinsuranceindepth.com, www.progressive.com, www.standardandpeers.com, Pact I Car Insurance

Vehicle (year, make, model, engine size) ______________________

Total miles driven in a year ______________________

Full- or part-time driver? ______________________

Driver's education completed? ______________________

Accidents or violations within the past three years? ______________________

Insurance company name ______________________

Agent's name, address, and phone ______________________

E-mail, website ______________________

Policy length

(6 months, 1 year) ______________________

| Coverage: | Premium | Premium | Premium |
|---|---|---|---|
| Bodily injury liability | | | |
| Per person | | | |
| $ | | | |
| Per accident | | | |
| $ | | | |
| Property damage | | | |
| Liability per accident | | | |
| $ | | | |

Collision deductible

$

Comprehensive deductible

$

Medical payments per person

$

Uninsured motorist liability

Per person

$

Per accident

$

Other coverage

Service charges

**Total Premium**

**What's Next for Your Personal Financial Plan?**

- Research actions you might take to reduce motor vehicle insurance costs.
- Talk to friends, relatives, and insurance agents to determine methods of reducing the cost of motor vehicle insurance.

# 10 Managing Risk: Health and Disability Insurance

## Affordable Care Act and You

Learning Objective: to look at different dimensions of the Affordable Care Act and the new healthcare exchanges.

1. Explain some of the issues that the Affordable Care Act set out to address.

2. What are some positive aspects of the Affordable Care Act?

3. What are some of the criticisms of the Affordable Care Act?

4. What is the maximum amount you will pay on your taxes if you don't have any insurance for a full year?

5. Using an online exchange estimator, fill out the below table assuming that you insure just yourself. Use an income of $100. List the costs for the bronze, silver, and gold levels.

| Level | Estimated Monthly Premium | Estimated Deductible | Estimated Out-of-Pocket Maximum |
|---|---|---|---|
| Bronze | | | |
| Silver | | | |
| Gold | | | |

6. Using the online exchange estimator, fill out the below table assuming that you insure a family with the following ages: 34, 37, 9, and 4. For this question use your school's zip code and state.

| Level | Estimated Monthly Premium | Estimated Deductible | Estimated Out-of-Pocket Maximum |
|---|---|---|---|
| Bronze | | | |
| Silver | | | |
| Gold | | | |

7. Using the same family as the previous question, calculate their Affordable Care Act subsidy assuming that they make $25,000 a year. Explain your results.

8. What would the expenses be for a single tobacco user who is 54 and living in Florida?

| Level | Estimated Monthly Premium | Estimated Deductible | Estimated Out-of-Pocket Maximum |
|---|---|---|---|
| Bronze | | | |
| Silver | | | |
| Gold | | | |

9. What would the expenses be for a single tobacco user who is 64 and living in Florida?

| Level | Estimated Monthly Premium | Estimated Deductible | Estimated Out-of-Pocket Maximum |
|---|---|---|---|
| Bronze | | | |
| Silver | | | |
| Gold | | | |

10. How much did changing the age alter the expected costs?

11. Explain what subsidies the above individual can expect?

12. What happens for the level of subsidies if the age is decreased to 54? 44? 34? Why do you think these changes occurred?

13. What happens to an individual's healthcare options when they reach retirement age?

## What do They Pay?

Learning Objective: to be able to calculate the out of pocket cost using several basic insurance plans.

For the purpose of this assignment, we will be using the three plans shown below. Assume that all of the medical expenses occur in the same billing year–so carry over the accounts from each previous year. With each situation, calculate what the individual would owe and find the important amounts to carry over to the next event. We will also assume that a doctor's visit only costs the co-pay. The plans shown below are gross simplifications of actual insurance plans so be careful when it comes to calculating your own medical expenses.

Plan A: Everything has a $20 co-pay. The plan has a $1,000 deductible but pays 100 percent of expenses after that. This plan also has a yearly limit on total deductible expenses of $2,500.

Plan B: Most things have a $10 co-pay. There is a $200 deductible with 80 percent coinsurance after that. There is no limit on yearly out-of-pocket expenses. There is a co-pay limit of $100 for the year.

Plan C: This is a health savings account. There is a $50 co-pay for everything and the account has $40,000 in it.

**1.** The whole household wants to play in a family kickball league so they need to get physicals. This ends up being five visits to the doctors' office. What was paid, and what is left? Show your work.

Paid by the plan Paid by individual Left

Plan A.

Plan B.

Plan C.

**2.** Kip sprains his ankle badly sliding into first base. This involves a doctor's visit along with an MRI which costs $3,000. What was paid, and what is left? Show your work.

Paid by the plan Paid by individual Left

Plan A.

Plan B.

Plan C.

**3.** Annalee has a baby. The total cost ends up being $15,000 along with the co-pay.

Paid by the plan Paid by individual Left

Plan A.

Plan B.

Plan C.

4. Everyone gets strep throat so this ends up being five doctors' visits.

Paid by the plan Paid by individual Left

Plan A.

Plan B.

Plan C.

5. Ahmed gets appendicitis. The surgery costs $12,000, but while he was in the hospital, he also got pneumonia. He had to remain hospitalized for 14 days at a cost of $200 per day. This also ends up being 3 co-pays.

Paid by the plan Paid by individual Left

Plan A.

Plan B.

Plan C.

6. Lee ends up getting a rare but treatable form of leukemia. He is hospitalized for several months and makes a full recovery. He total medical bills end up being $130,000 and one co-pay.

Paid by the plan Paid by individual Left

Plan A.

Plan B.

Plan C.

7. Summarize each plan in the table below:

Paid by the plan Paid by individual

Plan A.

Plan B.

Plan C.

8. Based on your calculations discuss as a group which plan you would expect to be most and least expensive. Explain your reasoning.

___

___

___

___

9. How much money would this family have needed to make to sustain them through this past year under each plan? A household this size would normally spend 4–10 percent of their income on healthcare. Explain your reasoning.

10. Why do most insurance plans require individuals to pay part of the cost of medical care?

11. Why do you think that health care is so expensive?

Name ______ Date ______ Class ______

# Assessing Current and Needed Health Care Insurance

**Purpose:** To assess current and needed medical and health care insurance.

**Financial Planning Activities:** Assess current and needed medical and health care insurance. Investigate your existing medical and health insurance, and determine the need for additional coverages.

**Suggested Websites & Apps:** www.insure.com, www.lifehappens.org, www.insurekidsnow.gov

Insurance company ______

Address ______

Type of coverage ☐ Individual health policy ☐ Group health policy ☐ HMO ☐ PPO ☐ Other

Premium amount (monthly/quarterly/semiannually/annually) ______

Main coverages ______

Amount of coverage for

- Hospital costs ______
- Surgery costs ______
- Physicians' fees ______
- Lab tests ______
- Outpatient expenses ______
- Maternity ______
- Major medical ______

Other items covered/amounts ______

Policy restrictions (deductible, coinsurance, maximum limits) ______

Items not covered by this insurance ______

Of items not covered, would supplemental coverage be appropriate for your personal situation? ______

What actions related to your current (or proposed additional) coverage are necessary? ______

## What's Next for Your Personal Financial Plan?

- Talk to others about the impact of their health insurance on other financial decisions.
- Contact an insurance agent to obtain cost information for an individual health insurance plan.

Name ______________________ Date ____________ Class ________

# Disability Income Insurance Needs

**Purpose:** To determine financial needs and insurance coverage related to employment disability situations.

**Financial Planning Activities:** Use the categories below to determine your potential income needs and disability insurance coverage.

**Suggested Websites & Apps:** www.ssa.gov, www.usa.gov/disability-benefits-insurance, www.dol.gov

37

YOUR PERSONAL FINANCIAL PLAN



## Monthly Expenses

| | Current | When Disabled |
|---|---|---|
| Mortgage (or rent) | $ ______ | $ ______ |
| Utilities | $ ______ | $ ______ |
| Food | $ ______ | $ ______ |
| Clothing | $ ______ | $ ______ |
| Insurance payments | $ ______ | $ ______ |
| Debt payments | $ ______ | $ ______ |
| Auto/transportation | $ ______ | $ ______ |
| Medical/dental care | $ ______ | $ ______ |
| Education | $ ______ | $ ______ |
| Personal allowances | $ ______ | $ ______ |
| Recreation/entertainment | $ ______ | $ ______ |
| Contributions, donations | $ ______ | $ ______ |
| **Total current monthly expenses** | $ ______ | |
| **Total monthly expenses when disabled** | | $ ______ |

## Substitute Income

| | Monthly Benefit* |
|---|---|
| Group disability insurance | $ ______ |
| Social Security | $ ______ |
| State disability insurance | $ ______ |
| Worker's compensation | $ ______ |
| Credit disability insurance (in some auto loan or home mortgages) | $ ______ |
| Other income (investments, etc.) | $ ______ |
| **Total projected income when disabled** | $ ______ |

If projected income when disabled is less than expenses, additional disability income insurance should be considered.

*Most disability insurance programs have a waiting period before benefits start, and they may have a limit on how long benefits are received.



## What's Next for Your Personal Financial Plan?

- Survey several people to determine if they have disability insurance.
- Talk to an insurance agent to compare the costs of disability income insurance available from several insurance companies.

# 11 Managing Risk: Life Insurance

## Shopping for Life Insurance

Learning Objective: to apply basic needs tools for life insurance and annuities.

The Porter family has two adults and three children. Mrs. Porter is a prominent lawyer in the state capital. Her income is currently $160,000. Her husband takes care of the kids. He has not worked in several years and has training as a computer programmer. Since he has not stayed up-to-date with best practices in his field, he expects that he would have a hard time if he ever tried to re-enter the work force. Their youngest child is 3 years old. They have the following outstanding debts: $140,000 on their mortgage, $20,000 on cars, $1,200 on credit cards, and $50,000 on student loans.

1. Given what you know so far about the Porter family, what is the most appropriate method for computing their life insurance needs? Why?

2. Using the most appropriate method, how much life insurance would you recommend the Porters purchase (show your work)? Are there any important additional considerations (if so adjust your recommendation accordingly)?

3. It is also very important to the Porters that their children receive a college education. Using a tax-exempt college savings plan, they have set aside roughly $10,000 for each of their children to go to college. They are on track to be able to save enough money for their children to go to college (an estimated $70,000 per child). What type of life insurance could they get to ensure that their children could still go to college in the event of the death of Mr. and Mrs. Porter? In order to meet just this goal, how much insurance do they need for the next 10 years? How much for the 10 years after that? How much for the 10 years after that?

4. The Camerones are both retired. They managed to run a highly successful nursery and want to pass it on to their children. The nursery covers almost 100 acres and is valued at $15,000,000. They are concerned over the fact that neither they nor their children have enough money to pay the estate tax. The estate tax rate is 45 percent on all assets transferred after the first $2,000,000. How much insurance do they need and what type of insurance is most appropriate?

5. Since their children are all out of the house, what is the most appropriate method to compute the insurance needs of the Camerones?

6. The Stoughtons are thinking about their retirement plans. They currently contribute the maximum tax-exempt amount to their retirement plans, but want to save even more for retirement. Explain several additional options that they could use to increase their income in retirement.

7. Mr. Zhao is looking at several different insurance options as an alternative to traditional savings vehicles. He has a stock mutual fund that averages an 11 percent return. In order to keep his family protected, he has decided that he needs to purchase additional life insurance. He has narrowed his shopping to two options: option 1 is term life insurance that costs $200 per month for 15 years and has no cash value, and option 2 is a life insurance product that costs $400 per month for 15 years and has an eventual cash value of $74,000. Both of these options will give the payout in the event of death. Which is the better option? Show your work mathematically and explain your results

## The Smiths and life Insurance

Learning Objective: use online services to shop for life insurance.

The Smith household now lives in Indanapolis, Indiana. They recently had a friend of the family pass away and realized how hard it would be to make ends meet after a death in the family. After doing some research, they have created the following criteria for their life insurance/annuity needs:

- The issuing company must have a physical presence in the ZIP code
- Mr. Smith is 35 and a SMOKER
- He is also OBESE
- They are hoping to get Universal Life Insurance
- A payout of $300,000.00
- They would also like to get an annuity with monthly payments of less than $20.00
- Since historically they have all gone to technical school/college/graduate school they would like to add something on to their main insurance needs so that their three kids can also have this opportunity

Find insurance quotes from two different companies that meet this family's preferences.

1. First insurance company:
2. Second insurance company:
3. Insurance policy(s) from the first company:
4. Insurance policy(s) from the second company:
5. Explain how you met all/most of this household's life insurance needs.

______________________________________________

______________________________________________

______________________________________________

______________________________________________

______________________________________________

6. What are the credit ratings of each of the companies that you chose (find company credit ratings from at least two different rating agencies)?

______________________________________________

______________________________________________

______________________________________________

______________________________________________

______________________________________________

**7.** What role does a life insurance company's credit rating play in the value of their insurance? What about the amount they can charge for insurance?

**8.** Research and find a life insurance company that has a credit rating lower than the above two companies. Why does the internet say that they have a lower than normal credit rating?

Name ______________________ Date ____________ Class ________

# Determining Life Insurance Needs

**Purpose:** To estimate life insurance coverage needed to cover expected expenses and future family livings costs.

**Financial Planning Activities:** Estimate the amounts for the categories listed below.

**Suggested Websites & Apps:** www.insure.com, www.bankrate.com/calculators/insurance/life-insurance-calculator.aspx

38 YOUR PERSONAL FINANCIAL PLAN

**Household expenses to be covered**

Final expenses (funeral, estate taxes, etc.) 1 $ ____________

Payment of Consumer debt amounts 2 $ ____________

Emergency fund 3 $ ____________

College fund 4 $ ____________

Expected living expenses:

Average living expense $____________

Spouse's income after taxes $-____________

Annual Social Security benefits $-____________

Net annual living expenses $____________

Years until souse is 90 $____________

Investment rate factor (see below) $____________

**Total living expenses** $____________

Total monetary needs (1 + 2 + 3 + 4 + 5) $____________

**Less:** Total current investments $____________

**Life insurance needs** $____________

**Investment rate factors**

| Years until spouse is 90 | 25 | 30 | 35 | 40 | 45 | 50 | 55 | 60 |
|---|---|---|---|---|---|---|---|---|
| Conservative investment | 20 | 22 | 25 | 27 | 30 | 31 | 33 | 35 |
| Aggressive investment | 16 | 17 | 19 | 20 | 21 | 21 | 22 | 23 |

***Note:*** Use *Your Personal Financial Plan sheet "Life Insurance Policy Comparison"* to compare life insurance policies.

## What's Next for Your Personal Financial Plan?

- Survey several people to determine their reasons for buying life insurance.
- Talk to an insurance agent to compare the rate charged by different companies and for different age categories.

YOUR PERSONAL FINANCIAL PLAN 39

Name ________________ Date ________ Class ________

# Life Insurance Policy Comparison

**Purpose:** To research and compare companies, coverages, and costs for different insurance policies.

**Financial Planning Activities:** Analyze ads and contact life insurance agents to obtain the information requested below.

**Suggested Websites & Apps:** www.insure.com, www.accuquote.com, Ladder, Lemonade, Fabric

| Your Age: | | | |
|---|---|---|---|
| Company | | | |
| Agent's name, address, and phone | | | |
| Type of insurance (term, straight/whole, limited payment, endowment, universal) | | | |
| Type of policy (individual, group) | | | |
| Amount of coverage | | | |
| Frequency of payment (monthly, quarterly, semiannually, annually) | | | |
| Premium amount | | | |
| Other costs:<br>• Service charges<br>• Medical exam | | | |
| Rate of return (annual percentage increase in cash value; not applicable for term policies) | | | |
| Benefits of insurance as stated in ad or by agent | | | |
| Potential problems or disadvantages of this coverage | | | |

## What's Next for Your Financial Plan?

- Talk to a life insurance agent to obtain information on the methods he or she suggests for determining the amount of life insurance a person should have.
- Research the differences in premium costs between a mutual and a stock insurance company.

# 12 Investing: Basics and Bonds

## Activity: Investing

**AS YOU READ,** learn the *vocabulary.* **AFTER YOU READ,** check your understanding through *Fact and Idea Review, Critical Thinking Questions,* and an *Extension Activity.*

### Understanding Your Investment Options

Life is full of risks such as illness, theft of property, and accidents that can negatively impact your finances. You can manage risk and protect your finances by avoiding risk, reducing it, accepting it, or transferring the risk to someone else.

For example, if you stop rock climbing, then your risk of injury drops to zero, and you are effectively avoiding that risk. The financial risk of a car accident can be transferred to the insurance company when you buy auto insurance. The risk of a fire in your home can be reduced by installing smoke detectors.

When you invest money, you want to minimize risk and maximize your **return.** If you buy a stock for $5 a share and sell it at $15 a share, your return is $10 on your original $5 investment. Some stocks may have a lot of **volatility**. You may buy a stock for $5 hoping it will increase to $20 over the next six months, but you watch nervously as the share prices spike, $3 one day, and then drop $5 the next. Some stocks have a lot of **risk** associated with them for that reason.

The level of risk, return, and **liquidity** you are comfortable with will dictate what investment and savings options you will use. Public utilities stocks, such as stock in a power company, are an example of a liquid investment. Homes, cars, and retirement accounts are not liquid, as they take time to be converted to cash. Having investments that are liquid allows you to access cash quickly. Of course, having some investments that are not easily turned into cash is good since you will not be tempted to cash them out.

Some examples of investments and their level of liquidity include:

- Certificates of Deposit (CDs) have a low risk and low return, and their liquidity can vary depending on the term of the CD. For example: a term of 3 months = moderate liquidity, while a term of 5 years = low liquidity.
- Savings accounts have low returns and low risks but are highly liquid, as you can access your money instantly.
- U.S. savings bonds and Treasury Bills, or T-Bills for short, are liquid but have a low return and low risk.
- Money market accounts have a low risk, moderate returns, and they are also highly liquid.

- Stocks in companies that are small and new will have higher risks and returns associated with them, whereas older, larger companies may have a lower risk and more moderate returns.

No matter what your preference is, it is wise to have varying levels of risk, return, and liquidity in your financial **portfolio** to protect you from large losses. You should not rely solely on high-risk, volatile stocks to meet your financial goals.

**Inflation** is another consideration when evaluating investments. Have you ever heard someone lament, "I remember when a loaf of bread only cost a quarter"? Inflation is a rise in prices of items over time, and deflation is the decrease in prices over time. Inflation erodes your purchasing power and can lower your investments' rate of return.

Cash investments such as stocks, bonds, mutual funds, real estate, and CDs are affected by inflation because fluctuating interest rates and prices are directly tied to their rate of return. If you spend $1,000 on a stock with a rate of return of 5 percent but inflation increases by 6 percent, you have lost $60 not gained $50 as would have been expected with no change in inflation. This is how inflation can chip away at your money. The U.S. treasury sells special bonds called Treasury Inflation Protected Securities (TIPS), and I Bonds that are adjusted to protect them from the effects of inflation.

You may need some help with creating a diversified portfolio. A financial planner or advisor can help, but it is important to choose the right one. Here are some ways to verify and evaluate the credentials of a financial planner or advisor:

- A certified financial planner (CFP) should be certified through the CFP Board of Standards, Inc., which you can verify on their web site www.cfp.net.
- Financial advisors should be registered with the Securities and Exchange Commission at www.adviserinfor.sec.gov.
- Financial planners and advisors should also be registered with the Financial Industry Regulatory Authority (FINRA) at www.finra.org.

### Vocabulary

**Return** the income that an investment produces

**Volatility** the degree to which an investment's return or value may change

**Risk** the possibility of variation in the return on an investment

**Liquidity** the ease with which savings or investments can be turned into cash

**Portfolio a** collection of investments

**Inflation** a general, prolonged rise in the price of goods and services

## Fact and Idea Review

1. How does inflation affect different types of investments?

2. What should you look for in a financial advisor's credentials?

3. How do risk, return, and liquidity affect savings and investment options?

## Critical Thinking

1. What are some effective risk-management strategies? How do these strategies protect against financial loss?

2. What is your risk tolerance? What investment options do you prefer? How does risk tolerance impact your decisions, and how can you manage risk?

## Extension Activity

Compare and contrast the risk, return, and liquidity of savings and investment options by creating a chart showing types of investments, and another chart showing savings account options. Research the investment options and savings accounts online.

| Investment Option | Description | Risk (low, moderate, high) | Return (percentage) | Liquidity (low, moderate, high) |
|---|---|---|---|---|
| Savings Bonds or U.S. Treasury Bonds (T-bills) | Nontransferable debt certificates, T-bills are issued by the U.S. Treasury | | | |
| Money Market Account | Savings account in which deposits are invested to yield higher earnings | | | |
| Certificate of Deposit (CD) | Issued to indicate money has been deposited for a certain term | | | |
| Savings Account | Money kept in a bank account | | | |
| Stocks<br>Type: | Ownership interest in a corporation | | | |

| Bank | Interest Rate | Balance Requirement | Accessibility |
|---|---|---|---|
| | | | |
| | | | |
| | | | |
| | | | |

## Ask the Experts

Learning Objective: to introduce students to a famous investor and their accomplishments.

1. What is the name of the investor your group is analyzing? ______

2. When and where was this person born? What kind of education did they receive?

3. What was this investor's investment strategy?

4. What did this investor invest in?

5. How much money did this investor start with? How much money did they make? What was their average return?

6. Did this investor draw any controversy? What were they accused of doing?

7. What advice does this investor have for individual investors?

8. If you were to make the same investment decisions as this investor, do you predict you would have the same outcome? Why or why not?

9. Are this investor's strategies still viable?

10. What influence did this investor have on society as a whole?

Name ______ Date ______ Class ______

# Establishing Investment Goals

**Purpose:** To determine specific goals for an investment program.

**Financial Planning Activities:** Based on short- and long-term goals for your investment program, enter the items requested below.

**Suggested Websites & Apps:** https://www.incharge.org/financial-literacy/budgeting-saving/how-to-set-financial-goals/, https://www.thebalance.com/setting-investment-goals-for-financial-independence-4120968





| Description of Investment Goal | Dollar Amount | Date Needed | Possible Investments to Achieve This Goal | Level of Risk (high, medium, low) |
|---|---|---|---|---|
| | | | | |
| | | | | |
| | | | | |
| | | | | |
| | | | | |



## What's Next for Your Personal Financial Plan?

- Use the suggested list in this chapter to perform a financial checkup.
- Discuss the importance of investment goals and financial planning with other household members.

41

YOUR PERSONAL FINANCIAL PLAN

Name ______________________ Date ____________ Class ________

## Assessing Risk for Investments

**Purpose:** To assess the risk of various investments in relation to your personal risk tolerance and financial goals.

**Financial Planning Activities:** List various investments you are considering based on the type and level of risk associated with each.

**Suggested Websites & Apps:** www.fool.com, https://investor.vanguard.com/investing/how-to-invest/investment-risk

### Type of Risk

| Type of Investment | Loss of Market Value (market risk) | Inflation Risk | Interest Rate Risk | Business Failure Risk |
|---|---|---|---|---|
| High risk | | | | |
| Moderate risk | | | | |
| Low risk | | | | |

### What's Next for Your Personal Financial Plan?

- Identify Current economic trends that might increase or decrease the risk associated with your choice of investments.
- Based on the risk associated with the investments you chose, which investment would you choose to attain your investment goals?

Name ______________________ Date ____________ Class ________

# Evaluating Corporate Bonds

**Purpose:** To determine if a specific corporate bond can help you attain your financial goals.

**Financial Planning Activities:** No checklist can serve as a foolproof guide for choosing a corporate bond. However, the following question will help you evaluate a potential bond investment.

**Suggested Websites & Apps:** http://finra-markets.morningstar.com/BondCenter/Default.jsp, https://finance.yahoo.com/





1. What is the corporation's name, website address, and phone number?
2. What type of products or services does this firm provide?
3. Briefly describe the prospects for this company (include significant factors such as product development, plans for expansion, plans for mergers, etc.).

## Category A: Bond Basics

4. What type of bond is this?
5. What is the face value for this bond?
6. What is the interest rate for this bond?
7. What is the dollar amount of annual interest for this bond?
8. What is the current price for this bond?
9. What is the current yield for this bond?
10. How often are the interest payments made to the bondholders?
11. Is the corporation currently paying interest as scheduled? ☐ Yes ☐ No
12. What is the maturity date for this bond?
13. What is Moody's rating for this bond?
14. What is the Standard & Poor's rating for this bond?
15. What do these ratings mean?
16. Is the bond secured with collateral? ☐ Yes ☐ No
17. Is the bond callable? If so, when?

## Category B: Financial Performance

18. What are the firm's earnings for the last year?
19. Have the firm's earnings increased over the past five years?
20. What are the firm's projected earnings for the next year?
21. Do the analysts indicate that this is a good time to invest in this company? Why or why not?
22. Briefly describe any other information you obtained from Financial Industry Regulatory Authority (FINRA), Moody's, Standard & Poor's, or other sources of information.

### A Word of Caution

The above checklist is not a cure-all, but it does provide some very sound questions that you should answer before deciding to invest in bonds. If you need other information, *you* are responsible for obtaining it and for determining how it affects your potential investment.

## What's Next for Your Personal Financial Plan?

- Use the suggested listed in this chapter to perform a financial checkup.
- Discuss the importance of investment goals and financial planning with other household members.

# 13 Investing: Stocks

## Common Stock, Preferred Stock, and IPOs

Learning Objective: to compare the risk and return of several equity investments.

1. What is the maximum return you can earn by purchasing common stock? What is the minimum return you can make?

2. What are the maximum and minimum returns on a preferred stock investment?

3. What is an IPO?

4. Who gets the money raised in an IPO?

5. Who gets paid when you buy common shares of stock online?

6. Suppose that Company A has paid a small dividend every quarter for several decades. Yesterday, Company A announced that they will no longer be paying dividends. What would you expect the stock market to do in reaction to this news?

7. Rank common stock, preferred stock, and IPOs in order of risk, from least risk to greatest risk. Explain your decision.

8. Why would you want to invest in more than one stock at a time?

9. You hear the following statement on the news: "You lose a little money every time you trade." What does this describe?

10. Company B has invested an enormous amount of money in environmentally responsible projects and reducing its own pollution. Company C has decided that they will only reconsider their environmental impact if one of their practices is illegal. Which company would you invest in? Why?

11. Which of the companies in the previous question presents the greatest risk, and why?

12. Which of the companies in question 10 should generate a higher return for their shareholders?

## Contrasting Stocks and Bonds

Learning Objective: to give a deeper understanding of the differences between asset classes.

1. Do stocks or bonds generally have a higher return? Why?

2. Although it is uncommon, every year companies go bankrupt. What happens to a company's stocks and bonds when it goes bankrupt?

3. Based on your understanding of stocks and bonds, which one would give better protection from inflation?

4. If you have high risk tolerance, would it be better to invest in stocks or bonds?

5. How could bonds be used to provide regular income? What if they don't pay dividends?

6. How could stocks be used to provide regular income? What if they don't pay dividends?

7. Is it uncommon for the stock market to lose 30 percent of its value quickly?

8. Is it uncommon for the bond market to lose 30 percent of its value quickly?

9. Many times during a market downturn, investors move toward safer investments (this is called "flight to quality"). If we think about investors within bond markets, how would we expect this movement toward safer investmens to affect markets?

10. If we have a "flight to quality" within stock markets, how would different types of stocks be affected?

**11.** How would a "flight to quality" move investments between stock and bond markets?

**12.** Does the stock market move up and down with the bond market? Why or why not?

Name ______ Date ______ Class ______

# Evaluating Corporate Stocks

**Purpose:** To identify a corporate stock that might help you attain your investment goals.

**Financial Planning Activities:** No checklist can serve as a foolproof guide for choosing a common or preferred stock. However, the following questions will help you evaluate a potential stock investment. Use stock websites on the Internet and /or library materials to answer these questions about a corporate stock that you believe could help you achieve your investment goals.

**Suggested Websites & Apps:** valuelin.com, finance.yahoo.com, morningstar.com

43

YOUR PERSONAL FINANCIAL PLAN

### Category 1: The Basics

**1.** What is the corporation's name?

______

**2.** What are the corporation's website address and telephone number?

______

**3.** Have you read the latest annual report?

☐ Yes ☐ No

**4.** Have you looked at information about this company on the Securities and Exchange Commission website at www.sec.gov?

______

**5.** What information about the corporation is available on the Internet?

______

**6.** What types of products or services does this firm provide?

______

**7.** Briefly describe the prospects for this company. (Include significant factors such as product development, plans for expansion, plans for mergers, etc.)

______

### Category 2: Dividend Income

**8.** Is the corporation current paying dividends? If so, how much?

______

**9.** What is the dividend yield for this stock?

______

**10.** Have dividends increased or decreased over the past three years?

______

**11.** How does the dividend yield for this investment compare with other potential investments?

______

**Category 3: Financial Performance**

**12.** What are the firm's earnings per share for the last year?

**13.** Have the firm's earnings increased over the past three years?

**14.** What is the firm's current price-earnings ratio?

**15.** How does the firm's current price-earnings ratio compare with previous years price-earnings ratio?

**16.** Describe trends for the firm's price-earnings ratio over the past three years. Do these trends show improvement or decline in investment value?

**17.** What are the firm's projected earnings for the next three years?

**18.** Have sales increased over the past five years?

**19.** What is the stock's current price?

**20.** What are the 52-week high and low prices for this stock?

**21.** Does your analysis indicate that this is a good stock to buy at this time?

**22.** Briefly describe any other information that you obtained from Value Line, Yahoo! Finance, Morningstar, or from other sources of information.

## A Word of Caution

When you use a checklist, there is always a danger of overlooking important relevant information. Quite simply, a checklist is a place to start. If you need more information, you are responsible for obtaining it and for determining how it affects your potential investment.

## What's Next for Your Personal Financial Plan?

- Identify additional factors that may affect your decision to invest in this corporation's stock.
- Develop a plan for monitoring an investment's value once a stock is purchased.

Name ______________________ Date ____________ Class ________

# Investment Broker Comparison

**Purpose:** To compare benefits and costs of different investment brokers' services.

**Financial Planning Activities:** Compare the services of an investment broker based on the factors listed below.

**Suggested Websites & Apps:** www.brokerage-review.com, www.stockbrokers.com, www.fool.com/the-ascent/buying-stocks/best-online-stock-brokers-beginners, www.finra.org

| | **Broker Number 1** | **Broker Number 2** |
|---|---|---|
| Broker's name | | |
| Brokerage firm | | |
| Address | | |
| Phone | | |
| Website | | |
| Complains filed with the SEC or Financial Industry Regulatory Authority (Answer Yes or No) | | |
| Amount required to open an account | | |
| Information and research services offered | | |
| Minimum commission charge | | |
| Commission on 100 shares of stock at $50 per share | | |
| Fees for other investments:<br>- Corporate bonds<br>- Government bonds<br>- Mutual funds | | |
| Other fees:<br>- Annual account fee<br>- Inactivity fee<br>- Other | | |

## What's Next for Your Personal Financial Plan?

- Using the information you obtained, choose a brokerage firm that you believe will help you achieve your investment goals.
- Access the website for the brokerage firm you have chosen and answer the questions listed in the section *Should You Use a Full-Service or a Discount Brokerage Firm?* in this chapter.

# 14 Investing: Mutual Funds and Alternative Investments

## Investing for Retirement

Learning Objective: to have students give basic financial advice on preparing for retirement.

1. What is retirement?

2. Suppose you want to have a yearly income of $50,000 in retirement. You expect to live 25 years in retirement and your inflation-adjusted rate of return on your safe investment is 3 percent. Estimate how much money you must save for retirement in order to have this consistent income. What are some issues that could cause your estimate to deviate in a way that could negatively impact your retirement fund?

| N | I/Y | PV | PMT | FV |
|---|---|---|---|---|
| | | | | |

3. For the past 15 years, Mr. Rodriguez has been saving 12 percent of his $45,000 annual salary for retirement. Initially, he planned to invest all of his money in medium-risk stock mutual funds that have an annual inflation-adjusted return of 10 percent. How much money has Mr. Rodriguez saved for retirement so far? Use monthly compounding and payments.

| N | I/Y | PV | PMT | FV |
|---|---|---|---|---|
| | | | | |

Mr. Rodriguez wants to have $1.5 million saved by the day he retires. If he has 20 years left until retirement, is he on track? Show your work below.

| N | I/Y | PV | PMT | FV |
|---|---|---|---|---|
| | | | | |

Suppose Mr. Rodriguez wants to take a little less risk, so he is now splitting his money between a bond mutual fund and a stock mutual fund. This change will lower his return to an average of 7 percent. How much will he have in retirement at this rate, given what he has saved and earned so far?

| N | I/Y | PV | PMT | FV |
|---|---|---|---|---|
| | | | | |

Clearly, Mr. Rodriguez needs to save more money to reach his retirement goal. How much more as a percentage of his salary does he need to save?

| N | I/Y | PV | PMT | FV |
|---|---|---|---|---|
| | | | | |

What percentage of his salary is this monthly payment, ignoring taxes?

4. Most wealth advisors recommend reducing your investment risk as you move closer to retirement. What advice would you give the individual in the previous problem about when it would be a good idea to begin investing in safer asset classes?

5. Mrs. Bouchard is trying to decide when to retire. Her social security benefits will be $1,500 per month in retirement. Let's suppose that she could start receiving these benefits today. How much would she need to have saved up in order to receive a monthly income of $4,000? Use an inflation-adjusted discount rate of 13 percent. and assume that she needs this monthly income for the next 35 years.

| N | I/Y | PV | PMT | FV |
|---|---|---|---|---|
| | | | | |

How much will she need to have saved without her social security?

| N | I/Y | PV | PMT | FV |
|---|---|---|---|---|
| | | | | |

# Getting the Nguyens Invested

Learning Objective: use online services to shop for investment options.

The Nguyen household is trying to find a good investment to add to their portfolio. They have compiled the following list of characteristics that are important to them. Use online tools to find three mutual funds that closely fit the Nguyen family's criteria. They want the following:

- Want to invest in Conservative Funds
- Prefer Class B shares
- Must have 1, 2, 5, years since inception

Try to find investments that meet all or most of the Nguyen family's preferences.

1. Fill out the table below with information on your recommended mutual funds.

| Characteristic | Option 1 | Option 2 | Option 3 |
|---|---|---|---|
| Fund Name | | | |
| Fund Ticker Symbol | | | |
| YTD Returns | | | |
| 1-Year Returns | | | |
| 3-Year Returns | | | |
| 10-Year Returns | | | |
| Lifetime Average Returns | | | |
| Inception Date | | | |
| NAV | | | |
| Expense Ratio (Net) | | | |
| Expense Ratio (Gross) | | | |
| Portfolio Net Assets | | | |
| 12 Month Low | | | |
| 12 Month High | | | |
| Minimum Investment | | | |
| Top Holding | | | |
| Percent in Top Ten Holdings | | | |
| Current Fund Manager | | | |
| Fund Management Group | | | |

2. Describe the strategy of each fund based on the information you found online.

Option 1 ________________________________________________

________________________________________________

________________________________________________

________________________________________________

________________________________________________

________________________________________________

Option 2 ________________________________________________

________________________________________________

________________________________________________

________________________________________________

________________________________________________

________________________________________________

Option 3 ________________________________________________

________________________________________________

________________________________________________

________________________________________________

________________________________________________

________________________________________________

3. Which option would you recommend for the Nguyen? Why?

________________________________________________

________________________________________________

________________________________________________

________________________________________________

________________________________________________

________________________________________________

Name ______________________ Date ____________ Class ________

# Evaluating Mutual Fund Investment Information

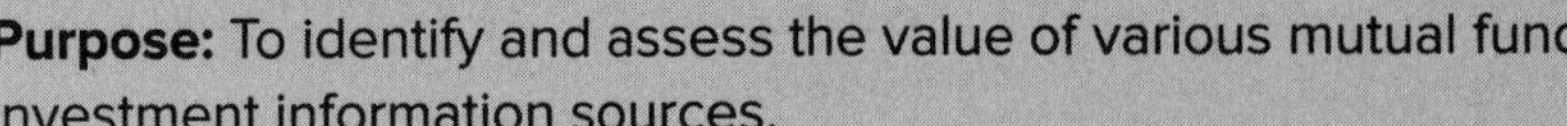

**Purpose:** To identify and assess the value of various mutual fund investment information sources.

**Financial Planning Activities:** Obtain samples of information that you might consider to help guide you in your investment decisions.

**Suggested Websites & Apps:** www.moringstar.com, www.kiplinger.com, www.imealliance.com

| Evaluation Criteria | Source 1 | Source 2 | Source 3 |
|---|---|---|---|
| Information Source | | | |
| Website | | | |
| Overview of information provided (main features) | | | |
| Cost, if any | | | |
| Ease of access | | | |
| Evaluation<br>• Reliability<br>• Clarity<br>• Value of information compared to cost | | | |

## What's Next for Your Personal Financial Plan?

- Talk with friends and relatives to determine what sources of information they use to evaluate mutual funds.
- Choose one source of information and describe how the information could help you achieve your investment goals.

Name ______________________ Date ____________ Class ________

# Mutual Fund Evaluation

**Purpose:** No checklist can serve as a foolproof guide for choosing a mutual fund. However, the following questions will help you evaluate a potential investment in a specific fund.

**Financial Planning Activities:** Use mutual fund websites, investment company websites, professional advisory services, and/or library materials to answer these questions about a mutual fund that you believe could help you achieve your investment goals.

**Suggested Websites:** www.morningstar.com, finance.yahoo.com, www.marketwatch.com

46

YOUR PERSONAL FINANCIAL PLAN



## Category 1: Fund Characteristics

**1.** What is the fund's name? What is the fund's ticker symbol?

______________________________

**2.** What is the fund's Morningstar rating?

______________________________

**3.** What is the minimum investment required by this fund?

______________________________

**4.** Does this fund have a history of paying income dividends and capital gain distributions?

☐ Yes ☐ No

## Category 2: Cost

**5.** Is there a front-end load charge? If so, how much is it?

______________________________

**6.** Is there a contingent deferred sales load? If so, how much is it?

______________________________

**7.** How much is the annual management fee?

______________________________

**8.** Is there a 12b-1 fee? If so, how much is it?

______________________________

**9.** What is the fund's expense ratio?

______________________________

## Category 3: Diversification

**10.** What is the fund's objective?

______________________________

**11.** What types of securities does the fund's portfolio include?

______________________________

12. How many different securities does the fund's portfolio include?

13. How many types of industries does the fund's portfolio include?

14. What are the fund's five largest holdings?

**Category 4: Fund Performance**

15. How long has the fund manager been with the fund?

16. How would you describe the fund's performance over the past 12 months?

17. How would you describe the fund's performance over the past 5 years?

18. How would you describe the fund's performance over the past 10 years?

19. What is the current net asset value for this fund?

20. What was the high net asset value for this fund over the past 12 months?

21. What was the low net asset value for this fund over the past 12 months?

22. What do the experts say about this fund?

**Category 5: Conclusion**

23. Based on the above information, do you think an investment in this fund will help you achieve your investment goals? ☐ Yes ☐ No

24. Explain your answer to Question 23.

### A Word of Caution

When you use a checklist, there is always a danger of overlooking important relevant information. This checklist is not a cure-all, but it does provide some very important questions that you should answer before making a fund investment decision. Quite simply, it is a place to start. If you need other information, *you* are responsible for obtaining it and determining how it affects your potential investment.

## What's Next for Your Personal Financial Plan?

- Identify additional factors that may affect your decision to invest in this fund.
- Develop a plan for monitoring an investment's value once a fund is purchased.